THE PUBLIC MAN

THE
PUBLIC
MAN

AN INTERPRETATION OF
LATIN AMERICAN
AND OTHER
CATHOLIC COUNTRIES

Glen Caudill Dealy

The University of Massachusetts Press   Amherst, 1977

Copyright © 1977 by Glen Caudill Dealy

All rights reserved

Library of Congress Catalog Card Number 77-1423

ISBN 0-87023-239-8

Printed in the United States of America

Designed by Mary Mendell

Library of Congress Cataloging in Publication Data

appear on the last printed page of this book.

TO
BERYL CROWE
AND
DEBORAH DEALY-BROWNING

CONTENTS

The specific forms of the thought of an epoch should not only be studied as they reveal themselves in theological and philosophic speculations, or in the conceptions of creeds, but also as they appear in practical wisdom and everyday life. We may even say that the true character of the spirit of an age is better revealed in its mode of regarding and expressing trivial and commonplace things than in the high manifestations of philosophy and science.

Johan Huizinga, *The Waning of the Middle Ages*

PREFACE

Not all books need prefaces, and I'm not certain that this one does. A common reason for a preface is to allow an "authority" to introduce a neophyte to a skeptical public. Here, however, the prefacee has already won his spurs with his widely read essays on the Latin American political tradition, while any spurs the prefacer may have won by addressing the themes of this book are long since tarnished. A preface is also useful when a book presents arcane data of momentous significance or else a seemingly bland text that is pregnant with implication. Glen Dealy's prose is neither arcane nor bland. His title and subtitle advertise what he's up to, and, to make matters even clearer, his introduction flags seven equivocations regarding Latin American political culture that he aims to rectify in succinct, explicit, and no-nonsense fashion. Professor Dealy's choice of the number seven ensconces him in an honorable tradition of Hispanic sociopolitical numerology stretching from the thirteenth-century law code of the *Siete Partidas* to the "seven essays" of Mariátegui and the "seven fallacies" of Stavenhagen.

Let me commence my supererogatory assignment, then, in a mood of self-indulgence. After I began teaching Latin American and European history in 1949, I was soon aware that the usual categories for explaining Latin American politics were sadly inadequate and that the political historiography of the region was often suffused with Anglo-American normative judgments. From my European readings it was further apparent that certain classical thinkers, neglected in my own country, seemed to speak directly to the Latin American experience. I refer in particular to the Thomistic legitimation for political order and the Machiavellian agenda for times of systemic breakdown. In an essay published in 1954 I proposed that Latin American political history seemed to place the Thomistic moment and the Machiavellian moment in contrapuntal relation. At the time I scarcely imagined how heavily Thomism had stamped early modern Iberian political thought; nor did I realize how strenuously Iberian scholastics had resisted Machiavelli's precepts. My scheme was paradigmatic and not historically anchored.

A decade later I undertook a Latin American chapter for Louis Hartz's *The Founding of New Societies* (1964). By now I had dipped into the scholastics and found that the neo-Thomism of Suárez was no mere residual legacy but was tailored to the political sociology of early modern Spain. Indeed, certain of his notions—the organic conception of society, the tension between popular sovereignty and delegated power—are today still germane to the polity in Latin America. I also discovered that Suarezian doctrines and Iberian political practice closely echoed Weber's ideal type of the patrimonial state. (I had not yet come across Raymundo Faoro's *Os donos do poder* of 1958, a pioneer application of the patrimonial construct to Brazil.) The late John Phelan chided me for too sweeping a use of patrimonialism and pointed out that a given situation reveals complex transactions among the several Weberian categories. He properly reminded us that a unitary model, insofar as a "model" pretends to simplified description, is valueless for discriminating among the host of Latin American cases. I employed the patrimonial type, however, largely to point up shortcomings of the term "feudalism" that is often applied to colonial Latin America and was even favored by my own editor, Louis Hartz. Moreover, if by "model" we mean not simplified description but an ideal type—a "stylization," or a tendency never wholly exemplified—the patrimonial construct is not without heuristic value. I think here of recent research on nineteenth-century Brazil that documents the selective resistance of patrimonial to legal-bureaucratic orientations, or the "baseless triangle" that has been posited to describe the political organization of modern Peru.

When hopes for democratic modernization in Latin America faded in the 1960s and authoritarianism reasserted itself in diverse forms, academics were driven to hypothesize a family of corporatist "models" that would help to differentiate such cases as the Mexican, the Brazilian, the Peruvian, and the Argentine. Some place this family within a "distinct" Iberian political tradition; others, like Glen Dealy in this book, assimilate it to a larger genealogy of "Catholic" polities; still others make it an instance of a widespread "corporatist" phenomenon that crops up irrespective of cultural or religious determinants. Any of these perspectives can be useful. The choice depends on *what* one wishes to elucidate and in what context. My own interest has centered on the specifically Iberian tradition—not as it might be manifested in "models" of social and political organization but as it persists in premises of belief that find a wide gamut of expressive form over the centuries and enter into myriad collisions and compromises with impinging ideological and industrial imperatives. I concluded the essay for the Hartz volume by suggesting five such orientations that appear to characterize Latin American polities of whatever hue or stripe.

The contrast between the United States and Latin American political traditions loomed large in my mind at the time of these essays, and I was encouraged to explain it—more simplistically than I might today—by differences between the political cultures of the Protestant and Catholic worlds. Again Weber helps us, for not only did he furnish transcultural political models, but he also canvased the belief systems of world religions for primary cues to social organization and economic behavior. His *Sociology of Religion* is quite as helpful for analyzing structure and process in Latin American societies as are his ideal types of political legitimation.

Here of course is where Glen Dealy's book comes in. He too has been struck by correspondences between political behavior and "cultural ethos" in Latin America. His search to define this ethos leads him, as his title states, beyond the region itself to "other Catholic countries." This brings him to accept an interpretation of Weber that makes capitalism an expression of the Protestant ethic and causes it to function as a "culture-integrator." By defining capitalism as a self-contained style of life rather than an institutional expression of a universalist ethic, he is able to propose that capitalism is not an inevitable stage of history and that the "bourgeois-industrial" ethos need not everywhere supplant what is loosely termed "traditional." He then posits a political culture of *caudillaje* (an "ethos propelling men in an unending, insatiable quest for public influence") as having prevailed in the Catholic West since the Renaissance. This culture, he insists, is not custom-bound and is quite as "rational" as capitalism, in that persons who seek to prove their excellence by its criteria do so in a manner as rational as that of the Yankee capitalist who amasses and reinvests wealth by Ben Franklin's maxims. The seeming particularism and affective behavior of caudillaje culture are therefore mobilized to accumulate political power much as the "Protestant" ethic of thrift and pecuniary calculation is employed in amassing capital. Thus Professor Dealy counterposes the political entrepreneur, or "surrounded man," of caudillaje culture to the economic or financial entrepreneur of capitalist culture. If the latter lives by the precepts of Ben Franklin, the former lives by those of Machiavelli. This theme has been developed, of course, in institutional rather than sociopsychological terms by those many historians who have explained that "bourgeois" economic power was subordinated to political or bureaucratic power in the late-medieval Iberian peninsula and subsequently in the American colonies. Professor Dealy, however, is less attracted to explanations deriving from institutional history than to those from cultural anthropology. His treatment subjects us to the shock of cultural recognition rather than to guarded inferences drawn from comparative historical analysis.

I leave the reader to savor the ingenious juxtapositions of observed behavior and philosophic matrix sprinkled throughout this book. He will find it tightly organized, written in a crisp, engaging style, and argued without jargon or disclaimers. The succulent footnotes ranging from Aristotle to contemporary fiction and social science are an adventure in themselves. The author presents a thesis to challenge political scientists as well as a patterned array of caudillaje behavior traits in a tradition of comparative cultural anthropology dating from the 1940s. If he slights the secular processes that shaped and sustained these traits, he shows unusual historical sensitivity when, in the third chapter, he removes us to medieval Europe and Renaissance Italy to reveal their prototypical expression.

Let me now enter a parting caveat about Professor Dealy's pan-Catholic scope. He links, as I said, caudillaje culture to all Catholic societies, and passes off economic "rationality" as a Protestant, capitalist culture trait. Yet if the Iberian lands have been able to fend off the incursions of Protestantism (save for the wildfire spread of popular cult groups in our time), they have almost equally resisted internalizing the experimentalism and scientific rationality that found such congenial inspiration in the bosom of Catholic culture (Machiavelli, Galileo, Descartes). It is one thing to speak of the organizing motifs, or "rationales," of Protestant and Catholic cultures, which permit one to contrast the United States and Latin America much as Ruth Benedict did the Zuni and the Kwakiutl. Weber's "rationalization," however, refers to something other than code and style of behavior. It designates an orientation rooted in the scientific revolution and in an originally theological quest for new modes of certitude. While some cultures are more hospitable to the spirit of rationalization than others—and

Catholic cultures vary in this regard—this spirit is inherently ecumenical and transcultural. Professor Dealy offers a sensitive delineation of a political culture (I would say, a preeminently Iberian political culture) on which we know the universalist spirit to be impinging with ever greater intensity. He judiciously leaves the reader to surmise the transactions and accommodations arising from this confrontation.

RICHARD M. MORSE

INTRODUCTION

This book can be read as a manual on how to take and hold power in Catholic countries. That was not my intent in writing it. But I have often been accused of having done just that by Latin Americans who have heard the essence of this work through public lectures. (Perhaps "accuse" is too strong a word as I have invariably been besieged after such lectures with requests for copies of the book in Spanish.) It has been suggested that like Machiavelli I have taken the view from the mountaintop in order to better recognize the salient topographical features of the plains, and analyzed the peaks from the perspective of the valleys. That methodological attribute can be taken as a compliment. Yet some might go so far as to attribute sinister motives to the author, seeking to find in my words a subtle support for or against Catholicism, Communism, the Right, the Left, Protestantism, or imperialism. To all such charges I plead innocent. I have neither sought nor found a "prince" or a cause to whom I might dedicate this essay in order to win favor for myself or power for practitioners of the ethos herein outlined.

If I have written a successful composition it must be attributed to observation of actual situations rather than to any *ought* statements. For I have endeavored to describe how power in fact is gained within Latin America and other Catholic countries while paying very little attention to who has it at the moment or will have it tomorrow.

My object in writing this book has not been to contribute to the struggle for power in Latin America but rather to elucidate the methods of combat, the weapons utilized. The work, then, is rooted in observation: my own and others'. In these pages I have sought to record the internal functioning of a culture. Therefore, numerous examples from published sources have been employed.

First and foremost this book endeavors to *describe* behavior in Latin America and other Catholic countries. I have tried to provide a descriptive model of everyday life in countries whose tradition is monolithically Catholic. Students South and North, Peace Corps volunteers, AID technicians, padres, and scholars have variously asked over the years for my interpretation of Latin American culture. My uniform response has been in terms of a description of actual behavior in that area of the world. If one cannot give examples of personal conduct within a region or country, I would maintain, he can know very little about that entity.

What one describes, however, must be chosen with care. Too often North Americans look to Latin America from the vantage point of neither its mountains nor its valleys but from their own charts and graphs of foreign investment, economic criteria such as GNP and per capita income, or perhaps a diagram of governmental powers based upon constitutional provisions. All of these may have their place. But they tend to be based upon comfortable analogies to our own economic and political system. The frequency with which United States investment of foreign aid must be turned around in the light of "change" in that area suggests that our descriptive models are lacking—for taking a long view, any observer would have to conclude that Latin America is one of the most stable areas of the modern world. Only surface elements seem to change.

Description of Latin America, to be meaningful, must be rooted in cultural observation on the broadest scale. We should seek to find a pattern of behavior in everyday lives that holds, whatever the GNP; whether the Fascists, the democrats, or the Marxists are in power; whether student riots are commonplace or seldom occur. This, because we know that in our own country a turnover in political parties, economic fluctuation, or a rise in per capita income has more often than not an amazingly minuscule influence upon everyday patterns of behavior. North Americans are basically energetic, conscious of time, work oriented, egalitarian, consumption directed, etc., etc., without regard to changes in the larger society.

It is the daily habits and world view of peoples living in monolithic Catholic countries that I would record. Alexis de Tocqueville constitutes for me the scholarly ideal type. In his profound analysis of American culture it was the ordinary behavior of countless individuals that impressed him most. And on the basis of this everyday activity of citizens he fashioned one of the most insightful theories ever made of our civilization. Taking a similar general orientation—however much the effort suffers in the comparison—I have endeavored to contribute to the understanding of Latin America through a descriptive analysis of the peoples of that area.

Secondly, the work attempts to *explain* behavior. After outlining a descriptive model of life south of the border, I have sought to provide an explanation for such activity. What force drives these people to behave in this manner? While beginning with Latin America, I soon found that any convincing explanation would have to range further than the area itself. Patterns of behavior can best be understood, I believe, by looking for a cohesive cultural ethos. And in this case the culture appears to be considerably broader than Latin America per se. Concluding that the explanation lay in Catholicism, I extended my research into the behavioral practices of other monolithically Catholic countries. Thus, the book came to be not only an enquiry into Latin American culture but an investigation drawing upon other culturally similar areas as well.

Thirdly, the work implicitly denies the validity of most current explanations for Latin American "problems." These various explanations, arising out of one culture and transposed onto another, seldom ring true to native Latin Americans. While sometimes used by them in the verbal battle against the Colossus of the North, such interpretations of Catholic culture often appear to miss the mark. Following are some of the more important misinterpretations.

1. *Latin American behavioral habits are more random than our own.* This work attempts to convince the reader that the life of the average Latin American is every bit as structured, defined, and integrated as, for example, that of the busiest New Yorker. There is a pattern to their lives which makes most citizens as "locked in" and predictable as their North American counterparts.

2. *Latin American life is irrational—that is, the average Latin American's behavior is inconsistent given his various life goals.* The pervasive North American bias suggesting that a little more attention to time and a bit more persistence on the part of the Latin American would allow him to "get ahead" in the world will be discredited in these pages. My view is that life in Catholic countries moves as rationally in terms of their goals as does our own.

3. *Latin America is a reflection, however pale, of North American society in its orientation toward personal autonomy.* I have shown elsewhere that the ideological and constitutional roots of Latin America are not copied from North America. Here I will endeavor to demonstrate the very fundamental disparity in cultural attitudes toward individualism as well.

4. *Latin America rests upon a vast "culture of poverty."* Put forth by Oscar Lewis and others, this thesis suggests that poverty determines behavior among the lower class. Instead, I advance the hypothesis that Catholic culture cuts across class lines: the behavioral attributes of that culture are as common among the lower class as among the upper class.

5. *Latin America is a "revolutionary society."* Literally hundreds of books have been written about Latin America in the past twenty years proclaiming the imminence of mass revolution. That premise is usually tied to the supposition that

6. *Latin America rests upon socioeconomic exploitation of the many by the few.* This book will deny these easy premises, maintaining that exploitation (excessive power over one's fellowman) characterizes Latin American society at all levels. Exploitation cannot be traced or attributed to any particular class. Consequently, to speak of a "revolutionary society" is largely nonsense. Whatever changes take place in power distribution will scarcely matter. Nowhere can one find glimpses of latent revolution in the fundamental sense. Agrarian reform will not, as is often suggested, enhance "the possibilities for genuine political democracy" (Robert J. Alexander, *Agrarian Reform in Latin America* [New York: Macmillan, 1974], p. 105).

7. *Latin American and Hispanic culture traits are unique to or at least reserved to "Romance language" or Latin culture.* Although conflicting somewhat with premise 3 above, this belief is widely held. Here I will endeavor to persuade the reader that Catholicism, not language, constitutes the common denominator of the culture I am describing.

Perhaps enough has been said by way of introduction. In the following pages I attempt to place these misinterpretations within the perspective of a wider cultural ethos.

THE PUBLIC MAN

I

THE SPIRIT OF CAUDILLAJE

Some years ago I traveled across the United States with a group of Latin American graduate students. Like Tocqueville and Beaumont, we visited churches, schools, country fairs, Fourth of July celebrations, and so on. As leader of this "see America" program, I suffered stress every morning over what could only be termed a clash of cultures. My problem stemmed from the fact that we were traveling by motor coach, and each evening the driver had to be informed as to the appropriate time to pick us up at the motel on the following morning. Departure time varied depending upon the day's schedule. From the first day of the trip we had trouble with this arrangement. Invariably, few students would have appeared by the announced time of departure.

Various remedies were tried such as group discussions of what we would miss if we did not leave at such-and-such a time, canceling of some early morning appointments, and my telling the group we needed to depart our motel earlier than we in fact had to leave. All schemes met with extremely relative success. One morning late in the tour and forty-five minutes behind the day's schedule, I asked the roommate of a yet-to-appear and perennially tardy student, "Why can't your friend ——— get up in the morning?" The ensuing conversation went somewhat as follows:

"Oh, he doesn't have any trouble getting up in the morning!"

"Then why isn't he down here?"

"He *wants* to be late."

"You must be kidding me."

"No, as a matter of fact, he gets up earlier than most people. He has been up for over two hours now. He's just waiting."

"Just waiting?"

"Sure. Every morning on this trip he has gotten up before I did. He always gets dressed and then just waits."

"What is he waiting for?"

"For everyone else to come down to the bus. He wants to be last."

"But why would he want to be last? Doesn't he know everyone else will be waiting for him?"

"Sure he knows. *That is why he comes down late!* The president never enters until his cabinet is assembled."

Let us assume—what I have since concluded—that this student's attitude toward the use of time is ideal-typical of men living in monolithic Catholic cultures. This conversation suggests that the late-arriving student possessed a highly rational view of time and space. Here is no picture of Pedro under the cactus oblivious to all except sunup and sundown; nor is this a picture of the "traditional society"—so dear to the hearts of social scientists—which defines itself by a primitive indifference to the division of the hour into minutes and seconds. Rather, we are here privy to a late arrival tied to a calculated use of time. Behavior is not random with this individual. He was *always* late, and, as I noticed after this conversation with his roommate, no matter what the announced time of departure he was late, within a minute or two, by the same amount of time.

If one wishes to argue that this student's behavior is rational, it is not enough simply to show that his actions contain a pattern. Rationality cannot be discussed apart from the goals of one's actions. Concisely stated, to social scientists rationality means behavior that is consistent with goals. And, one may legitimately ask, "What life goal could possibly be compatible with a consistently tardy appearance in motel lobbies across the country?" Hopefully, the answer to that question can be found in the subject matter of this book, for we are here concerned with human behavior and the reasons for that behavior.

To say that most of the Western world during the last three centuries has been dominated by capitalism as a way of life appears self-evident. (I am using *capitalism* here as Weber employed the term, that is, "to denote a whole pattern of civilization" and not simply a mode of economic exchange.)[1] Even though Marx gave the word a pejorative meaning, no one seems to dispute the historical fact of capitalism. This is a more recent view than is sometimes realized,[2] and yet when Max Weber first wrote his essays in 1904–05 which later became known as

The Protestant Ethic and the Spirit of Capitalism his readers were on the whole self-consciously aware of the phenomena under discussion. It was the question of the *causality* of capitalism, not the fact of capitalism, which drew the attention of men like Sombart, Troeltsch, Brentano, and Tawney.

In this book I am concerned both with the description of a way of life and with a causal explanation for that life. The task is thus doubly difficult, as the life style here described has not been usually viewed as other than a remnant of the past, a way of life that is in transition to some "higher" form of existence, namely, industrialism and its attendant values.

It is the argument of this book that capitalism does not hold a unique place within the Western world as a culture integrator. Nor do the values of capitalism stand at some teleological apex of civilization toward which all peoples must move or are moving. This latter perspective, I believe, rather reflects the particular stance of bourgeois man: the economists and social scientists that capitalistic society has fostered.[3] Such egocentricism must be not only denied in the realm of social theory and in the name of the sociology of knowledge but also denied in empirical fact. Marxists err in making capitalism an inevitable, albeit not final, stage of history; social scientists err in holding to a view of society which can be summarized without too much unfairness as modern-bourgeois-industrial-urban *vs.* traditional. The interpretation of capitalism as an exclusive mode of existence tied to rational economic activity is here being challenged. It is not a unique and inexorable life style toward which all societies are moving.

Out of the Renaissance era arose a style of life which I have labeled *caudillaje* (cow-dē-ya′-hay)—from the Spanish word *caudillo.* Caudillaje designates in ideal-typical fashion a life style oriented toward values of public leadership. It embraces a concept of man personified as a leader in a public setting. The word itself may be defined as the "domination (*mando*) or government of a caudillo." But we are not here speaking of political leaders per se, but of a style of life according to which everyman attempts to be a leader or caudillo: a caudillo in the sense given the word by the *Diccionario enciclopedico ilustrado de la lengua española* (1953) as "one who, as head (chief) and superior, guides and commands people." [4] The word itself is unimportant other than as a means of discussing the life style of a people—a life style oriented toward the goals and values of public leadership.[5]

What must be insisted upon is the rational quality of activity in caudillaje society. Caudillaje man, or the "public man" as I shall alternately call him, lives a life of rule-bound behavior. His acts contribute to his goals, and it is this which sets caudillaje society apart from other, more primitive patterns of behavior. History as sometimes written is little more than a struggle of men for public power. Yet what has usually been lacking in such struggles is an internalized code guiding personal behavior: a value frame directed toward the goal of becoming a public man.[6] Historically men have sought public power through class prerogatives, heredity, force, wealth, divine intervention, or a combination of these features. But in the Western world since the Renaissance we have seen the development of what might be termed, to parallel Weber, a "spirit" of caudillaje. That is, we are considering a rational culturewide ethos propelling men in an unending, insatiable quest for public influence. Seldom, if ever, have whole nations followed an ethos of leadership where everyman aspires to public power; where the logic of the ethos produces a nation of leaders without any followers.[7]

This spirit of caudillaje pervades those areas of Western Christendom that have remained monolithically Catholic in culture since the Renaissance. Most obvious in fitting that description are Spain, Portugal, Italy, Spanish and Portuguese America, and to a lesser extent Hungary, Ireland, France, French Canada, Austria, Romania, and Poland. Caudillaje is not a phenomenon reserved to a particular time period in a nation's history, for example, Renaissance Italy with its condottieri or nineteenth-century Latin America with its colorful caudillo presidents.[8] Nor is caudillaje related to specific groups within these geographical units, for example, Renaissance princes or Latin American gauchos. No culture of poverty or of affluence separate from the larger society can be found.[9] Rather, there lives a pervasive culturewide phenomenon of caudillaje which dominates every level of these societies and every facet of human behavior. One thinks, then, of "everyman" when referring to a "spirit of caudillaje." My thesis is that from the lowly cobbler to the caudillo-president there exists a common uniting value frame—that it would be as egregious an error to separate the values of political leaders from those of political followers in those areas of the world as it would be to sever the world outlook of nineteenth-century robber barons in the United States from the Horatio Alger values of the "common man" in this country at that time.[10] Caudillaje men are public men, men who may or may not become leaders in fact. Edmundo Desnoes, a Cuban author, expresses this truism when he writes of José

Martí and Fidel Castro: "They are public men who have surrendered themselves to a cause." [11] The cause, in other words, is secondary; their public nature constitutes the given.

Observation of these monolithic Catholic societies shows that they are characterized by a value structure that supports the goal of becoming caudillos or leaders. Catholic man is public man. He defines himself in terms of a code of excellence that derives (originally) from the public or political sphere. He thinks, acts, and has his being within a framework of public values. If one looks at the fabled man-on-the-street in these areas of the world, one will find that he is endeavoring to act in a manner which he believes consistent with the way a public man would (should/does) act. Statements such as the following should be accepted in light of this truth. "A Spaniard will always sacrifice his desire for wealth or comfort to idealistic motives of pride or glory no matter how vain they may be." [12]

From other caudillaje societies have come similar observations, and such behavior becomes intelligible once the public standard of activity is perceived. Yet, as we shall find, pride and glory cease to be "idealistic" once their public content is assessed.

But while these men take their orientation from public values, they may often shy away from public participation in a formal sense. In many a town or village across the caudillaje landscape, political offices go begging for want of candidates. This is because real power may be only slightly related to the holding of designated formal positions. In such cases it is possible to have "massive indifference to public life, and a mobilization of egos and ambitions" exist side by side.[13] By definition, then, a public man is a leader.[14] We are defining a mode of behavior that is elitist. While asserting that Catholic culture exhibits a pervasive value system extending to all levels of society, it is not contradictory to also contend that in a qualitative sense we are examining an elitist value system and code of ethics which is at once democratic in its pervasiveness and indifference to class barriers and elitist in content. As one author summarizes, "it is no good putting on airs in Ireland, for everyone is very subtly putting on airs." [15] Referring to the behavior of Spanish men on a train, another author writes: "They behaved with ease as people who live by custom do; and they gave an impression of an aristocratic detachment. This is true of all classes from the rich to the poor, who have the same speech and the same manners. There are no class accents in Spain worth mentioning; there are only the regional variants of speech. . . . [The Spaniard] is, he has always been, a hidalgo—a *hijo de algo*—a person of some consideration. And upon this consideration, however impalpable it may be, the very beggar in the streets reposes."[16]

To see the Catholic world as grounded in a haphazard struggle for power among contending opponents would miss the unique character of caudillaje society. Catholic man has been extremely rational and his behavior highly ordered with regard to achieving his end of public power. This makes him "a very rational, cautious, and prudent man, and frequently a very worried one." [17]

The behavioral response of Catholic man to this problem of taking and holding power is as direct and as rational as was Protestant man's response to the question of making money. Weber performs an injustice to Catholic man when he stresses the rationality of Protestants over Catholics. His error was to compare *medieval* Catholics with *modern* Protestants, omitting to survey post-Renaissance Catholicism except in the economic sphere. Weber does not see rational action in the medieval world. Since he saw medieval economic activity as essentially nonrational, and therefore noncapitalistic, he appears to have extended his thinking to Catholic society in general. Consequently, he can refer to the "planless and unsystematic character of Catholic man." [18] What social scientists have not always realized is that when Weber argues, "the most important opponent with which the spirit of capitalism . . . has had to struggle, was that type of attitude and reaction to new situations which we may designate as traditionalism," [19] he is counterposing traditionalism to capitalism in much the same way as one might demonstrate the retarding effect of Hinduism upon capitalism.[20] For example, Weber later shows traditionalism to be embodied by "a man [who] does not 'by nature' wish to earn more and more money, but simply to live as he is accustomed to live and to earn as much as is necessary for that purpose." [21] Yet what is readily observed in the case of Hinduism, for instance, but not seen in the example of "traditionalism" is that it can constitute an alternative ethos and not merely a foot-dragging backwardness. One suspects that in the minds of most social scientists "traditional society" and "backward society" are synonymous merely because the latter does not possess the social scientists' capitalistic value bias.[22] We must go further, however, and try to understand cultures within their own value framework. Post-Renaissance Catholic culture is very far from the custom-tied behavior which Weber perceived in medieval Europe.

Weber's error tended to be exacerbated by Schumpeter's belief that "capitalism develops rationality." While Protestant rationality does hold in the realm of economics, in terms of public action it is the Catholics who have been more rational in pursuing their ends. In each case, men seek to demonstrate their excellence in terms of the ultimate criteria of their respective societies. Protestant man sought to be privately saved; Catholic man *qua* man sought to be publicly virtuous.

The essential differences between Protestant rationality and Catholic rationality are two: (1) Protestant man has been primarily rational in the economic sphere and has only derivatively used the same rationality within the political world, while Catholic man has been primarily rational within the political sphere (political action is as "unclean" for Protestant man as economic action is "unclean" for Catholic man); and (2) Protestants had no historically developed and religiously derived framework for the rational achievement of their goal of wealth (salvation), while Catholics did possess such a theoretical structure for the rational achievement of their goal of public power. A discussion of the first point constitutes the subject matter of this chapter while the second point will be elaborated upon in chapter 2.

Catholic man pursues public power the way Protestant man strives for private wealth. In the one context there is a political referent for life's activities, in the other an economic referent. Both world views generate extremely rational worldly activity. One might ask, for example, what are the functional equivalents within caudillaje society for capitalist man's economic virtues of hard work, frugality, and reinvestment of capital? Immediately come to mind the virtues of leisure, ostentation, and instant gratification through the spending of one's capital. In short, I will argue that the latter virtues are equally as rational for caudillaje society as the former are for capitalistic society.

We are focusing here upon the accepted rational means for gaining public power and for gaining wealth: in the case of caudillaje man certain agreed-upon, essentially public or political virtues are demanded; for capitalist man, certain agreed-upon economic virtues emerge. Both fulfill the function of personal self-realization. And each carries its own "signs" or "indicators" of individual excellence which are readily recognizable by both pretenders and observers within their respective social orders. While not all capitalists who aspire to become millionaires act with equal talent, so too not every would-be caudillo aspiring to become a Machiavellian "New Man" possesses equal ability. Yet all participate inside the ethical boundaries of their respective cultures. Caudillaje man seeks public acclaim for public deeds. The feats which he attempts are calculated to bring this approval every bit as much as the bourgeois-capitalist calculates his entrepreneurial dealings in such a way as to produce economic profit. The following statement is not, I feel, too atypical of caudillaje man's attitude toward saving, self-indulgence, and work. Implicit is an admiration for a life of publicly displayed gentility. Long since separated from its religious roots, here is an account of the caudillaje life style:

> If I have ten pesos in my pocket, and feel like having a sweet, I'll buy it, even if my other expenses are not taken care of. So that I won't be left with just my desires, eh? I hate to deny myself little things.
>
> I have often asked myself, what is worth more at the end of one's life, the things one has accumulated or the satisfactions one has experienced? I believe that human experience is worth more, no? And although I have worked all my life, now, when I want to go somewhere, I go in a taxi. I never travel in a bus.
>
> If I go into a restaurant, I don't order beans. I order a fried steak or a couple of eggs. If I want to sit down, I sit; if I don't feel like getting up in the morning, I sleep. Yes, the best heritage I can leave my children is to teach them how to live. I don't want them to be fools...I swear by my mother, I won't let them become ordinary workers.[23]

One can see from such a world view that to the degree that capitalism extends into caudillaje society "it *is* an invasion," as Haya de la Torre contended, "with its own particular characteristics, with its own particular politics, and with formidable social effects." [24] In short, it is antithetical to these societies.

Public power like economic wealth is rooted in rational accumulation. Capitalism measures excellence in terms of accumulated wealth; caudillaje measures one's virtue in terms of accumulated public power. While capitalistic man thus seeks to ensure his economic credit, "to secure my credit and character as a tradesman," as Ben Franklin said,[25] caudillaje man moves to secure his base of political credit, a "credit with the people," as Machiavelli phrased it.[26] It is certainly an unfounded prejudice that only liberal democracy rests upon this "credit" of the people. Machiavelli's *Il principe* attests on every page to the significance of such popular support.[27] The importance of power as a currency has been sketched within the larger social-political order by Karl Deutsch:

Power cannot be counted exactly, but it can be estimated in proportion to the power resources or capabilities that are visibly available, such as the numbers of countable supporters, voters, or soldiers available or required in a particular political context. Levels of intensity of support, of morale, of skills and resourcefulness, insofar as any or all of these can be estimated, may also be taken into account by appropriate weighing, much as manpower budgets or estimates of military forces can be at least roughly calculated. ... *Prestige is then to power as credit is to cash.* And physical force —enforcement in the narrow sense—is to power as gold is to paper money or to savings accounts and checks.[28]

One may refer to a contemporary example. In studies of motivation, David McClelland has perceived the differences in personal behavior that follow upon an individual's cultural needs. One should not confuse a need (n) for power with the need (n) for economic achievement (Ach), says McClelland, even though both may lead to assertive behavior. "The motivation of a person with high n Power is quite different; he wants to have impact on others, to control and persuade them. Whereas a businessman with high n Ach would do whatever is necessary to get his factory built, another man in the same position with high n Power might get so involved in controlling others and being the boss that he might not even care if the factory never got built." [29] And so it is with caudillaje individuals in general. The point being that a person who fails to opt for economic gain can still be highly motivated—he can pursue goals and utilize rational means to achieve these goals.

"Rational" friendship provides the roots from which springs public power. However acquired, one becomes rich in terms of public power by the number and quality (power) of one's friends.

He weakened himself by casting off his friends. . . .

Not having friends in the country . . . he was forced to accept what friendships he could find. . . .

Consider how little difficulty the king would have had in maintaining his reputation in Italy if he had observed the aforesaid rules, and kept a firm and sure hold over all those friends of his. . . .

He abolished the old militia, raised a new one, abandoned his old friendships and formed others; and as he had thus friends and soldiers of his own choosing, he was able on this foundation to build securely. . . .

I will only say . . . that it is necessary for a prince to possess the friendship of the people; otherwise he has no resource in times of adversity. . . .

One . . . who becomes prince by favor of the populace, must maintain its friendship, which he will find easy, the people asking nothing but not to be oppressed.[30]

In these phrases of Niccolò Machiavelli, the Ben Franklin of Catholicism, we see an already developed ethos of a world view according to which the goal of public power finds a rational means in the acquisition of friends. The currency of public power is friendship. For the public man friends are used as currency in the identical sense in which capitalists speak of money and currency as synonymous terms. Capitalism and the exploitation of man by man only became feasible with the introduction of currency. As John Locke so vividly reminds us, the accumulation of wealth was dependent upon the creation of this medium by which treasure might be laid up and passed on to one's heirs.[31] One should think of friendship in a parallel manner. Though perhaps sometimes less tangible than money in a bank, friends can be accumulated, saved, and spent in much the same way.

At another level of discourse what I am suggesting is that *particularism can be rational.* Talcott Parsons in constructing his influential pattern-variables, set "universalism" against "particularism" and, following Max Weber, claimed a certain rationality for the former over the latter. By universalism he meant that a person will apply a general standard in his relations with others, whereas in particularistic or traditional society man will respond to his fellowman on the basis of personal attributes or relationships. What Parsons and others failed to note is that caudillaje culture operates upon internalized codes or standards of behavior and that these standards require persons to respond to significant others in a wholly rational, patterned, nonrandom fashion.[32] Particularism, or more specifically, "friendship," does in fact, like universalism, demand general standards albeit not the standards of capitalist society.

The public man is dominated by a need to acquire friends. He undertakes this acquisition as the ultimate purpose of his life. The common man of caudillaje society knows that power depends upon friendship, that there are certain means of acquiring, holding, and losing friendship, and that without it one is lost. By contrast, the capitalist has no need for such interpersonal connections.[33] The marketplace reduced his relationships to a cash nexus, as Marx said, where not friendship but alienation would predominate. Adam Smith in *The Theory of Moral Sentiments* characterized this appropriate "go it alone" attitude of capitalists:

> It is a sedate but steady and faithful attachment to a few well-tried and well-chosen companions, in the choice of whom he is not guided by the giddy admiration of shining accomplishments, but by the sober esteem of modesty, discretion, and good conduct. But, though capable of friendship, he is not always much disposed to general sociality. He rarely figures in those convivial societies which are distinguished for the jollity and gaiety of their conversation. Their way of life might too often interfere with the regularity of his temperance, might interrupt the steadiness of his industry, or break in upon the strictness of his frugality.[34]

Laissez-faire, "to allow to do," can, significantly also be translated in the social sense as "to let alone." It is little wonder that we have now advanced from being lonely individuals to become a "lonely crowd," as Riesman suggests.

To maintain that caudillaje society finds its roots in friends rather than capital, is not, however, to deny them belief in the guiding influence of an unseen causal agent a la Adam Smith. The notion of a hidden hand is ever present within caudillaje culture. It usually is referred to as "fortune" or "destiny." "To me, one's destiny is controlled by *a mysterious hand* that moves all things," says the Mexican, Manuel Sánchez.[35] Invoking an implicit social Darwinism, he goes on, "only for the select, do things turn out as planned; to those of us who are born to be tamale eaters, heaven sends only tamales." [36] Manuel then demonstrates how the mysterious force works out economically: "Once I decided to try to save and I said to Paula, 'Old girl, put away this money so that some day we'll have a little pile.' When we had ninety pesos laid away, pum! my father got sick and I had to give all to him for doctors and medicines. It was the only time I had helped him, the only time I had tried to save. I said to Paula, 'There you are! Why should we save if someone gets sick and we have to spend it all!' *Sometimes I even think that saving brings on illness.*" [37] Giovanni Verga, portraying a Sicilian family in his classic novel, *I Malavoglia*, has 'Ntoni remark, "Isn't it just our luck to have to break our backs for other people? And then, when we've scraped a little money together, the devil comes and takes it away again." [38]

For the public man worldly success is directly correlated with his public power. And the test of public power is found in the extent of his friendships. Friendship, or *amicitia* as here used, does not pertain to sentiments of private congeniality[39] but functions as a weapon of power.[40] Personal relationships therefore must be cultivated, the circle of friendship extended. "Playing the friendship game" thus becomes a necessary way of life—as all-consuming as playing the money game within capitalistic cultures.[41] As one Venezuelan is recorded to have said, "I believe that the correct and exemplary life of the individual depends on the friends he chooses . . . on the opportune exchange of ideas and advice on both sides. . . . One often has friends whom one serves. At other times one demands to be served and is satisfied. I . . . have made a cult of friendship." [42]

Public power readily grows for those who already possess a sizable capital. "It takes money to make money" is a well-known truism of the bourgeoisie. So too for caudillaje man. His slogan becomes, "It takes friends to acquire friends." [43] Success breeds success. Followers go to the followed the way money and credit gravitate toward the rich. Public men know this and therefore endeavor to demonstrate to one and all the extensive nature of their existing friendships. It is necessary for one to appear successful. Hence, he must surround himself with friends, visible and invisible, in order to assist himself in still further accumulation. J. A. Pitt-Rivers observes,

> It is a commplace that you can get nothing done in Andalusia save through friendship. It follows then that the more friends a man can claim the greater his sphere of influence; the more influential his friends are the more influence he has. Friendship is thereby connected with prestige, and boastful characters like to assert how many friends they have, how extensive is the range of their friendships.[44]

Barzini gives some rules for survival if you are Italian:

> Rule One: choose the right companions. In order to succeed, a young man must not only join a large and powerful group but also, once in, worm his way to the top, become one of the influential elite, one of the leaders or even the solitary chief, if he can, in order to use the whole group to serve his own purposes. It is clearly impossible for any man to do so alone. He must have an *entourage* of his own; he must choose a smaller group inside the large group, join it, and eventually influence it.[45]

The public man strives to become the "surrounded man." To be surrounded with friends accomplishes for the common man of caudillaje society what a new car furnishes for the common man of capitalistic society. It is an objective sign of success. And the means of aggregating these persons no more enters the picture at the moment of this demonstration of importance and achievement than does the means of acquiring a new house or car for the capitalist. Both may indicate a lack of "good sense," a final exhaustion of effort. Friends, like cars, may be repossessed, will return to another power center tomorrow. But on the other hand, the show of added friends may contribute to yet other quite tangible gains of public power.

Caudillaje man can best convey the impression of being a successful public man by becoming the surrounded man. Everywhere one sees this surrounded man in caudillaje countries. From the extended family to the sidewalk coffee shops; from the sports palace to the national palace, one observes the phenomenon. Most of life is lived in a public forum and most of life is deliberately social.[46] In caudillaje culture men consciously seek out the center of activity as a desirable place to live, work, and enjoy oneself. For example, in a small Mexican town the central plaza attracts.

> It is the place with the most *movimiento*, the townspeople say, but the word means more than movement alone; it also signifies noise, people, and color—all things which are valued in the social side of Tonalá life. The area around the plaza is also more densely populated than the blocks around the edge of town. High value is placed on being in the center of *movimiento*, not only as a site for shops and businesses, but also for one's home. In contrast to our flight to the suburbs, the Tonaltecan wants to be where "life" is.[47]

One may suspect that the reason caudillaje culture is so loud, that radios usually blare, that stereos spin on full volume, is because the secularized public man must create an ambience of noise around him to simulate being in public, surrounded by people.

Unlike the capitalists, caudillaje men actively endeavor to aggregate friends. Life is organic rather than atomistic, as the medievalists would say. Indeed, one finds that caudillaje man avoids appearing alone in public as capitalist man avoids being idle in public. Friendship thus has the connotation of the Roman *clientes*. The number of hangers-on, the size of one's entourage, becomes an indication of one's public power.[48] Miguel Asturias in his novel, *El señor presidente*, demonstrates what it means to be at the pinnacle of power: "All those who recognize that you are worthy to be First Citizen of the Nation and who therefore surrounded you at that terrible moment, . . . surround you now and will continue to do so as long as it is necessary." [49]

Being surrounded in no way implies a communitarian ethos. An aggregation in caudillaje society almost invariably indicates a degree of organization and hierarchy. One day caudillaje man may pay deference to a friend who has invited him to dinner, and the next week that friend may in turn pay deference to him at a similar function which he in turn has arranged. What is important is that outside of the family, nay, even within the family, persons seldom meet as equals. Someone clearly takes the role of the surrounded man and the others assume the role of surrounders. By playing this game from an early age, caudillaje persons learn much about domination, subservience, and role playing in general.[50] With regard to role change, I am reminded of an AID-supported trip to the United States of a group of Latin American small-town mayors. They were to attend a conference on local government. In charge of the trip was a young caudillaje economist known for his easy-going, mild-mannered ways: on this all the North Americans who knew him were agreed. Thus it was with some consternation that the AID mission received a telegram on the second day of the conference from their United States hosts. How were they to deal with the young economist who had organized and totally intimidated the much older *alcaldes* to such an extent that only persons designated by him beforehand were allowed to ask questions or respond in any way to the conference presentation? In fact, the matter might have gone undetected by his hosts had not afternoon and morning speakers been switched on the second day of the conference—thus causing enormous confusion among the delegates with their previously rehearsed responses to specific lectures. Through the medium of interpreters this fact had not come through to some delegates, and questions were being asked about matters that had not yet been spoken!

Timeworn procedures exist whereby the public man can surround himself. Caudillaje society is systemic society. By systemic I mean what Italians term *sistemazione*. While it is difficult to convey the exact meaning of this concept—which can be extended to everyone and every level of society—an example is that of "the *bandito* Giuliano, who flourished in Sicily just after the war, gave proper military titles to his henchmen and was surrounded by a primitive but rigid etiquette";[51] or the young woman of poor family explaining her failure to marry by

stating there was not enough money available to *sistemare* her brother
and to provide her with an adequate dowry as well.[52] In other words,
caudillaje cultures are ordered, hierarchical, and "proper" in the sense
of conveying deference to whom deference is due. Such a quality lends
itself to maintenance of structures (after first establishing the institutional base) for gaining status through waiting numbers. By illustration, one of the more effective means a lawyer, professor, businessman,
civil servant, or military person may utilize for building a constant aggregation around his person and/or office is to (1) refuse to delegate
any responsibility, and then (2) become "inaccessible." One sees this
game played out in a hundred variations throughout caudillaje countries
in the smallest village as well as in the largest cities. Whether it be a
long line of *indígenas* waiting to see a *juez de paz* in an Ecuadorian provincial *aldea*, angry numbers seeking opera tickets in Milan, or an
American tourist endeavoring to settle a traffic violation in Madrid—
the same logic is being pursued by the *jefe*.[53] His importance increases
as the number of persons seeking his assistance, approval, help, or mercy
grows. As Ann Cornelisen writes of an Italian villager's return from
seeing a lawyer: "She was impressed. She said Don Peppino must be
very important because he had a big waiting room with chairs, lots of
chairs, and all of them were taken." [54] Another observant writer summarizes the theme:

> It is almost recognized as good form that a public official keep sub-
> ordinates and clients waiting far beyond their appointment time.
> Indeed, power is treated almost as if it were a kind of quality which
> needs to be displayed in order to validate it. Part of the style of
> politics is behavior that displays this quality; it can be used at any
> bureaucratic level. No matter where you stand there will be some-
> one sometime over whom you have power—whether you are the
> minister of state who casually keeps a waiting room perpetually
> full of petitioners, or the janitor who slams the gate just before
> closing time and opens it tardily in the morning.[55]

Such behavior is wholly rational given the goal of the public man.
That is, it achieves the end of surrounding one's office and person with
large numbers of people who in fact need him. Love for bureaucratic
procedures, elaborate hierarchies, inefficient secretaries, stamps, and
seals, all attest to the public man's desire to give the appearance of possessing special qualities by prolonging the matter at hand. Behaviorally,
then, one finds that it is not the "efficient" man who through hard work

has cleared his desk and seen all of his clients who is perceived as the man of excellence. In fact, efficiency is *counter*productive in terms of caudillaje values. It constitutes a public confession of one's lack of importance.

If one looks hard enough, in almost any office in caudillaje society one will find an unassuming man usually dressed in black who in fact understands how things are done and runs the day-to-day business of the office. His longevity in office is proverbial—in Guatemala he seems to survive all administrations from Communists to right-wing militarists. These men are, in short, unexpendable as, almost like the eunuchs of Roman bureaucracy, they appear to uniquely operate upon other than the values of the society in which they live. That is, at first glance they seem not to be "public men." Yet, as we shall see later, their hold upon true power places them well within the value frame of caudillaje society. Like Machiavelli, they are advisors to the power holders and by supplying continuity make governance possible.

It is, consequently, the surrounded man who is beheld as the man of virtue. Clients, therefore, are not persons to be taken care of and expedited on their way. Clients are to be savored, preserved about one's person. Thus, the later one arrives for an appointment, the more people who await one's entrance, then the more excellent one must be. And this kind of public virtue can be successfully sought and exercised in any size community. For example, professors in caudillaje society are usually late for class and often do not show up at all. When they do arrive tardily, their rage knows no end if the students have left. It is as if the knights would not await the king. His purpose in being late has backfired. Whence emerges the picture of a society wherein the conduct of each individual is minutely attuned to the disposition and behavior of others.

Luigi Barzini, in discussing the gestures of Italians, recounts the following scene which demonstrates the importance of being surrounded.

One of the most economical and eloquent of Sicilian gestures I saw one day in the lobby of the Hotel des Palmes, in Palermo. A man entered from the street. He obviously wanted everybody to know immediately, beyond doubt, that he was a gentleman, *un gran signore*, a man of means and authority, accustomed to being attended on. He looked around as if searching for a friend among the people loitering in the room, took off his overcoat, held it at arm's length for a fraction of a second, and without bothering to see whether a servant was at his side, dropped it. A real *signore* always has somebody ready to receive his coat when he takes it off. He never needs to check. The coat, of course, did not drop to the floor. A bellboy was there to catch it.[56]

In the same book, Barzini tells what happens to those young women who achieve their goal and become movie stars. In their success they act as all Italians would act: "They stop coming to Via Veneto, except two or three times a year, and then only surrounded by friends, photographers and women noticeably not half as beautiful as they." [57] Or yet another example of the importance of being surrounded elucidated by the same author: "Take the matter of theatre tickets. To pay the full price for a theatrical performance is equivalent to admitting that one is nobody, has no friends and enjoys no particular powers." [58] The same principle, of course, works for any bureaucratic procedure from fixing a parking ticket to getting an illegal import license. Those with friends have power, those without are considered and treated as nobodies.

Here lie tangible outward signs of public power which everyman can seek. The public man enhances his importance if he has a chauffeur to wait upon his needs. He must have attendants in the house to serve him and his guests. Servants must carry his children's books to the bus stop. Professors must have their guards and attendants; businessmen must have someone to transport their briefcases and parcels, mistresses to await their pleasure; and housewives must have their serving girls, laundresses, and cooks. This has not often been understood by foreigners. North Americans, for example, tend to see waste in the private chauffeur common to caudillaje society, or the maid who carries a child's books to the school bus. They fail to consider the positive implications that the use of retainers has in caudillaje culture. Serving persons enhance the self-esteem and need for status and deference of the consumer of these services in the same manner in which savings accrued through the dispensing with such services enhance the self-esteem and position of the capitalist. To see this plethora of attendants as merely an extension of an economic stage of a labor-intensive society would be to ignore social reality. An ability to purchase appliances, cars, and other gadgets of industrial civilization has had no discernible effect upon the demand for personal servants among those with an ability to pay.[59] The phenomenon seems to be more cultural than economic. It has often been noticed, for example, that among the lower classes there is also a great deal of maid and personal service. "The social decorum of even the most modestly-situated families requires the presence of a servant" [60] in Spain. Gavin Maxwell in *The Ten Pains of Death* records a Sicilian peasant: "We used to finish picking up the olives in the evening after sunset. They were all put into a sack which my companions took in turns to carry on their backs. I never carried it because I was the landlord." [61]

Some men in caudillaje society are born to a wealth of public power while most must strive for it. For the fortunate few, servants, chauffeurs, gardeners abound from childhood. Their parents have many friends—a life of power is secured, barring some unforeseen catastrophe or a great squandering of the public credit they have inherited. But for most the struggle for influence is real, pervasive, vicious, and all-consuming. Their resources of power are marshaled, saved, and spent in such manner as to enlarge their capital of public power.

The endeavor to surround himself occupies most of Catholic man's waking hours.[62] Such efforts are necessary not merely for ego fulfillment but also to achieve real ends. The surrounded man has at his fingertips vast resources of power and influence through his "connections." Those who are alone have very little to bank upon.

One of the prime methods by which these friends can be of help is through the phenomenon of intercession. Friends can intercede on one's behalf to accomplish almost anything. Without such intermediaries very little could be achieved. Catholic societies since medieval times have relied upon these agents to expedite one's interest. Today personalistic mediation constitutes one of the hallmarks of caudillaje culture and distinguishes it from the impersonal mediation of the marketplace economy and world view of capitalism. For Protestants intermediaries between God and man have tended to be economic due to the default of organized churches to fill the void of intercession thrown off at the Reformation. By contrast, caudillaje culture carries into societal life the notion of personal mediation found within its religious tradition.

In a study of St. Denis in French Canada one can perceive this analogous relationship. Men appeal to saints for religious intercession the way they appeal to "friends" to intercede upon their behalf for the accomplishment of this-worldly goals. The author of the study writes:

> As saints are obviously so potent, supplications constantly ascend to them. These prayers are usually directed to the saints and to the Virgin, although God may be prayed to directly, as in the *pater*.

The relationship between mortals and saints is much more intimate than between men and God. Saints are besought to intercede with God in the supplicant's behalf. This round-about method is explained thus: "Say that I know you and want to ask a favor of you. I can ask you directly, and you may or may not grant it. But if I know someone very well who knows you intimately, I can ask that person to ask you for me and I am more likely to be granted the request." [63]

Here one sees the advantage of being surrounded with multiple and overlapping friendships. "God" is usually inaccessible, taking a day off, short of money, and so on. But ask one of his saintly acquaintances who over the years has become your good friend—one who has presided over your wedding, birth of your children, one to whom you have made many offerings and sacrifices—and anything becomes possible.

The systemization of supplication has created what a Spanish author calls "the mendicancy of influence." Today, he says,

everything in Spain—access to employment, the concession for a business, the leasing of a flat, the installation of a telephone, the resolution of the most common bureaucratic requirement—is obtained because one has a friend. Of course, the immense majority of people don't have those friends who take care of things, but they can ask to borrow some from those who have mountains of them. With this a veritable traffic in favors has been unleashed upon us, a new and curious form of mendicancy, the mendicancy of influence, which ... brings, to those well endowed with contacts, a large clientele of hopeful or grateful supplicants.[64]

An example taken from a rural Italian study will elucidate how the process works. A young man wishes to become a military officer but has no outstanding military qualifications.

However, his father is a close friend of the mayor, and, when the young man is called before the enrollment board, he is provided by the mayor with a letter of introduction to the president of the board. As a result, the young man is told to present himself for the initial examination, and provided with a letter of introduction to the president of the examining board. He is duly accepted, and the "raccomandazione" originally given by the mayor is repeated by various links in the chain of military instructors, examiners, and superiors, throughout his course of training. He eventually gets his commission, and is posted to an infantry regiment in Venetia. In this case, the "raccomandazione" was powerful enough to ensure his getting the commission; but too weak to obtain for him a posting nearer home, or in one of the crack regiments. The boy writing home points out that a colleague of his who actually was less well placed in the final examination was posted to a crack regiment in Rome, where his family lived: but, he says, the latter was a "raccomandato di ferro" meaning that the influence brought to bear on his behalf was exceptionally strong.[65]

What merits emphasis in the phenomenon of personal intercession described is that "individuals forming the chain are anxious to oblige the person who was the last link, not the actual applicant who is unknown to them." [66] Caudillaje culture thus spins upon these letters of credit. The rational quality of the system overwhelms the social analyst. To function within such a culture, "living successfully," is contingent upon the influence of others. Certain worn and prescribed methods exist for gaining their accommodation.

The first means to power available to the public man is his family.[67] An orphan indeed presents a pathetic figure in this culture, as he is bankrupt at birth.[68] All others begin life "surrounded," if only by a mother. Those who have father, mother, and many brothers and sisters are almost assured of some success in life: they already have at least minimal power because they are surrounded by "natural" human resources which may be exploited. Additional power will come easier. Strength of family ties does not appear to be some quaint holdover from traditional times that disappears in Catholic societies with modernization. There are many indications that this institution continues to dominate the life of caudillaje man after a degree of industrialization has taken place.[69] One can with confidence predict that the strong family system will survive as long as caudillaje values prevail.[70]

Consider the extended family: that network of second cousins, godparents, and close friends of blood relationships. It surely survives because it rests upon the felt needs of everyone within the group. Family relationships and the *compadre* system of Catholic culture serve as a power base for each participant—it is his one constant and "free" aggregation.[71] Others must be earned. Interchangeably, each member of the family helps each other member toward the personal achievement of power.[72] This in contrast to the capitalistic loose family relationship according to which an endeavor to accumulate wealth may serve as a divisive rather than a unifying factor, particularly among the middle class. The closeness of families in caudillaje culture can therefore be explained in part as surviving out of individual self-interest while capitalistic families disintegrate for the same reason. In North America upper-class families often function as a unit while middle-class families do not. This may well be because the father in middle-class families can be of much less "use" to his children in their struggle for selfhood, status, and economic power than in the case of the upper-class family.[73] Also, it should be noted that within Catholic society children are useful to their parents in that a new child can bring in a new *compadre*. The circle of power thus broadens for the parents.

The extended family as the cornerstone of public power has most frequently been commented upon in relation to dictators. "The men whom caudillos call upon first will naturally be their relatives, because the ties of blood are the surest and the strongest." [74] "To the ties of blood can be added those which create a religious relationship between the compadres or godfathers ... and the relatives of the baptized as well as the child himself. These ties often remain powerful enough to oblige the partners to help each other in all circumstances." [75] What must be recognized, however, is that nepotism at the highest ranks of political power only reflects culturewide behavior. The nepotism of a Castro, a Batista, a Perón, or a Trujillo[76] does not simply represent the corruption of an economic, money-oriented behavior, as is so often assumed. Rather, their actions are typical of previous reliance upon friends and relatives and of an accepted mode of behavior that can be traced back to the very foundation of the society itself. For example, in Francisco Pizarro's tiny conquering army in Peru, men from Trujillo, Spain, occupied the first thirty-seven positions while the top five were held by Pizarro, his two bastard brothers, a half-brother, and a legitimate brother.[77] More recently, the former dictator of the Dominican Republic, Trujillo, by becoming the godfather of a great number of children performed on a large scale what the lowliest peasant does to ensure his future and the support of those around him.[78] Nor is it by chance that one of the best observers of modern Mexico describes that country as ruled not by any form of impersonal pluralistic competition but by what he terms "the Revolutionary Family." He argues that "the basic difference between Revolutionary governance and Porfirian governance is that Mexico now has a turnover in dictators every six years at the national and state levels and every three years at the local level."

It is a country, he says, where "there is no effective opposition or effective suffrage. Checks and balances, separation of powers and restraints by legislative and judicial agents are paper thin." Instead, Mexico's affairs are ordered "by the head of the Family, who is usually the incumbent President of Mexico, assisted by about twenty favorite sons." [79]

Just how important family may be to martial life can be seen in the following excerpt taken from John J. Johnson's work on the military in Latin America:

> The opportunities for one or a few families to control a service is illustrated by the situation in the Venezuelan Navy and Marine Corps. ... The Venezuelan Navy in 1962 had six admirals; two of them were the Larrazabal brothers, Carlos and Wolfgang; a third, Sosa Rios, was married to a sister of the Larrazabal brothers and a second Larrazabal sister was married to a commander in the marines, Oscar Nahmens. Also, the Carupano and Puerto Cabello revolts of mid-1962, led by the marines, tended to be family affairs. The Carupano uprising was headed by J. T. Molina, who "jumped the gun" on what was supposed to be a general revolt, when his brother, J. J. Molina, a high-ranking marine officer, was arrested for plotting. The same J. J. Molina is married to one of three Bermudez sisters, the other two of whom are also married to marine corps officers. Furthermore, Lieutenant Commander Morales, who deserted when the revolt broke out in Carupano but who returned to the barracks the night of the Puerto Cabello outbreak, is a brother-in-law of Lieutenant Commander Francisco Avilan, one of the navy officers who backed the marine uprising at Puerto Cabello.[80]

It is outside of the extended family that the attempt to surround oneself takes on a competitive nature. Schools, political parties, bureaucracies, barracks become battlegrounds in this endeavor. Caudillaje man enters into competition to surround himself with friends. By analogy, capitalistic societies have long been organized in such manner as to expedite the making of money. Wealth being the capitalist's prime goal, one finds societal and political arrangements so constructed that many may efficiently achieve their common end. This same efficiency in structured goal achievement is visible within caudillaje societies. Thus, while capitalistic countries established their stock markets to assist men in the accumulation of money, so caudillaje nations have institutionalized the means for the accumulation of friends.

For example, formal educational institutions do not exist to convey technical knowledge that will be economically useful, as in capitalistic cultures, but to provide a place where young men may begin to sort out and establish hierarchies of power. They prepare the youth for a lifetime of such activity. Barzini describes the process in Italy whereby "many boys acquire their wisdom in school: they learn how to get ahead smoothly, how to defeat rivals while retaining their friendship." [81] That takes skill. But from the streets of Milan it is only a small jump to a tiny agricultural village in the Bolivian highlands where social stratification turns upon one's decorum and the function of education is "to provide the basis for the manners thought of so highly by *gente buena*." Consistent with the ethos, education furnishes "the verbal and intellectual skills that are useful to *gente buena* activities," [82] not something as relatively worthless as improved knowledge of planting and harvesting. Students thus do not study so much as prepare a following, consolidate a power base. Often their instructors become pawns to be manipulated or discarded according to the dictates of political exigency.[83] From the professor's standpoint it is not the goal of teaching that determines behavior so much as aggregating followers to support his ends of public power whether that be in the form of a deanship, rectorship, or political party post. University clubs, elections, and protest movements in caudillaje culture are thus a microcosm of national life. Not only do they reflect a pervasive set of cultural values, they embody a process of socialization into the values of these societies. A student's ideology may overtly shift from Communism to Fascism between his university years and age thirty. But his goals of public power remain constant, and the process of aggregating friends, of becoming the surrounded man, goes on unabated. And, as we shall see later, the code of ethics which he has early embraced will probably not change with his shift of political allegiance from the Left to the Right. In fact, evidence indicates that the ideological gap between, for example, reactionary hacienda owners and their avowedly revolutionary Marxist opponents in Latin America often constitutes no greater disparity than that between conservatives and liberals in the United States.

National politics in caudillaje society is almost constantly in the hands of university graduates or the military. This has much less to do with a monopoly of coercive force than usually supposed. Rather, it follows from the fact that both university and barracks provide an ideal setting for the aggregation of a following which may sooner or later prove useful. Most personalized political parties in these areas can be traced back either to coteries of friends within the university and professional *colegios* or to military cliques. For this reason, the ambitious young man in caudillaje society does not begin his career by hawking newspapers or going "West." Instead he dons a tie and goes off to school aspiring to become a lawyer or a general—either may lead to the pinnacles of public power.

The public man's values are reflected in the type of organization he joins.[84] Throughout caudillaje society "brotherhoods" exist. While animal clubs (Elks, Lions, Eagles, etc.) with their atomistic, businessman, egalitarian, service-oriented nature characterize capitalistic society, so brotherhoods characterize caudillaje culture. They are often religiously oriented (for example, Opus Dei in Spain) or religiously related (Mafia in Sicily) and are always organic, elitist, and exclusive. Their unity derives from affective ties of brotherhood which have little to do with public "service" and much to do with building and appropriately displaying one's public image. Thus, since the Renaissance, literary *tertulias*, aristocratic clubs, and military cliques have existed in abundance wherein individual excellences might be appropriately displayed and aggregations solidified.[85] There is not, however, any of the fanatical joining of multiple groups which Tocqueville found in the United States. One who seeks power based on an individualized following cannot afford either to spread himself too thin or to align himself with groups whose membership might possibly conflict with his clientele in another public setting. As a consequence, the public man tends to concentrate on one organization, and very often this will be an informal "power behind the scenes" aggregation.[86]

One of the settings wherein individual qualities may be properly exhibited is the barracks. Universal to caudillaje society is a love for those attributes of the public man derivative of military life and organization: formalism in etiquette, speech, and dress. Deference can be secured through rank itself. The public man thus finds military existence very compatible once he removes himself from the bottom rung of the hierarchy; he then always has someone below to wait upon his needs. Hierarchy allows him to assume the role of public man. Naturally, then, an affinity for militaristic values can be seen everywhere within caudillaje society. Uniforms are worn by maids, school children, street sweepers, and guards as well as presidents, generals, and clergymen; deference is shown by everyone to his superior in the realm of physical, linguistic,[87] and ideological posturing.

What better organization could the mind of man contrive for the surrounding of oneself with "friends"? Martial life consists of advancement based upon an individual's performance before his fellowman as well as friendship, influence, and family. Opportunities for one to aggregate a following through the sole exercise of his public virtue are excellent. Bolstered by the hierarchy of rank, the man of aspirations can assure himself of a mass public and a mass following by concentrating upon the few: his fellow officers. No doubt this explains the affinity for military life of the ambitious enlisted men from the middle and lower classes. In the barracks they find that execution of public virtue provides opportunities for success which energetic young capitalists have traditionally found in the marketplace. Thus barracks revolts, coups, and countercoups often typify caudillaje society. The successes and failures of those revolts are the functional equivalents of the ups and downs of the capitalistic marketplace: they signal the building of empires and the periodic bankruptcies of these empires. Behind each "disturbance" lies a clash of two or more aggregations of men.[88] Hence, while caudillaje nations traditionally fight few wars and tend to lack international bellicosity, they have a singular emphasis upon the military order. What has been said of Machiavelli might be extended to the public man in general: "One suspects that he wants all the glory of arms without the sufferings of actual war." [89] But caudillaje militaristic activities hardly need such formal settings. The less polished ways of a Garibaldi or a Castro are more typical than those of the Peróns, the Francos, and the Mussolinis.[90]

Ideology is of secondary importance. Doctrinal content tends to be of less significance than the person espousing it throughout caudillaje society. Such propagandistic activity reflects within an organizational framework the values of a whole society. For example, a Venezuelan labor leader said in an interview:

What attracts one is the attention of a leader, the quality of the leader that wins over masses. Well, I was an admirer of (name) and if (name) had gone into the Communist Party perhaps I would now be a Communist or if he were from (party) I would also be in that party ... because it is only later that one begins to know party doctrine ... philosophy, programs, objectives. But first one is drawn by a man, and it is this same attraction that a labor leader may also have. (Workers) join a union out of sympathy and fondness for a leader who listens to them, who calls them.[91]

Militarism in capitalistic countries has traditionally been unimportant (for example, lack of large professional armies), while at the same time some of the finest munition makers come from these nations. Caudillaje nations, by contrast, continually emphasize militarism while appearing to be always deficient in the logistical supply and support for such activity. Yet these facts should come as no surprise. Caudillaje military organizations provide a means for individual self-realization within the traditional values of their culture. For these ends a ceremonial sword may be more necessary than an atomic bomb. Capitalistic nations who supply weapons to caudillaje states (for example, the Latin American nations) out of a hope that the military may become a modernizing force will most likely be disillusioned. Instead, these arms furnish the means for demonstrating personal heroics—it is not military defense but the individual's opportunity to surround himself with public glory that captures his imagination. And, parenthetically, when capitalist nations sell their military hardware, they are also trucking in the Protestant production ethic. Two cultures thus lock themselves in a grotesque dance of death—each achieving its goals through an international division of labor.

National bureaucracy is another setting that furnishes structure for the aggregation of followers. The "goals" of the organization are usually secondary. For the participant it provides, rather, a vehicle for aggregating friends, making "connections," and serving to enlarge his power base. In all likelihood the very utility of the civil service accounts for the fact that within caudillaje countries, even in an age of organization, there exist disproportionately big bureaucracies, just as the military organizations and especially the officer corps within these nations are inordinately large. The bureaucracy necessarily operates as a catering service to caudillaje man's pursuit and demonstration of his ability *tener muñeca* ("to have connections"), *tener palanca* ("to have leverage"), or *tener cuello* ("to have pull"). In performing their function, correctly understood, these organizations move faultlessly.

Bureaucracy within caudillaje culture functions with supreme rationality. Given the public man's goals of deference and respect based upon control over other persons, the interminable delays, stamps, "procedures," giant logbooks, and so forth, become perfectly logical. Capi-

talists see nothing but "backwardness," "underdevelopment," "ineffi-
ciency" in such procedures. Yet on an individual basis the bureaucrat
of caudillaje culture is achieving in the same sense that the impatient
capitalist is achieving. From the psychological aspect, the capitalist's
abrasiveness and impatience says, "I have self-worth because I represent
such and such a company and I am entitled to service." The caudillaje
person says, "I have self-worth because I am in charge of these stamps
and forms and I will exact your deference on that basis the way you
would exact deference on the basis of your wealth and economic position."

For the capitalist, authority finally has its roots in competence.
Max Weber saw in bureaucracy this legal-rational authority following
upon one's competence in his assigned task. (Weber derived the notion
from his familiarity with the German-Lutheran concept of "calling.")
Caudillaje culture, however, rests upon the rational use of power rather
than legality. Yet such is the force of the concept of legal-rational
authority that it has now become popularly assumed that any society
whose bureaucracy is founded on other than technical competence cannot be authoritative. Such a perspective fails to take into account caudillaje culture as other than a remnant of the past.[92] Erich Fromm typifies this position: "*Rational authority* has its source in *competence.* ...
it is always temporary, its acceptance depending on its performance."
Fromm then adds, "the source of irrational authority ... is always
power over people." [93] I believe, on the contrary, that power over
people is the central ingredient of all types of authority, both rational
and "irrational." What Fromm and others have failed to realize is that
competence can be other than of a technological or of a formal
bureaucratic nature.[94]

Competence forms the basis for authority within caudillaje society,
and this competence has its grounding in a wholly rational life. Behavior comes tied to a rational calculus of means adapted to ends. Without a high level of individual competence the aggregation of a following would be impossible; and without a following, authority becomes
impossible. Even more in caudillaje than in capitalistic culture does
rational authority rest upon a competence whose acceptance is, as
Fromm said, "depending on its performance."

Common errors of capitalistic man arise from a mistaken impression of what he is seeing when he looks upon caudillaje society. Consider for example the statement of a Uruguayan, trained in the language and concepts of Talcott Parsons, writing about his own country:

It is clear that particularism is a very important phenomenon in Uruguayan society and it prevails over universalism. A great number of facts support this. It is well known that the prevailing system of selection for government employees is based on kinship, on membership in a certain club or political faction, on friendship, etc. These are all particularistic criteria. A similar phenomenon is present in private enterprise where selection of personnel on the basis of particularistic relations is very common. The use of universalistic criteria, such as the use of standardized examinations is exceptional. Quite frequently when such universalistic criteria seem operative, they are applied to candidates who have been previously selected on the basis of personal relationships.[95]

The average person from capitalistic society who reads these words will at least unconsciously reject the Uruguayan system as being tied to an intolerable randomness under which one's life chances are inexorably related to the power and position of his economic heritage; a society in which not only individual merit but graft, corruption, nepotism determine all. In short, it appears to be a situation in which "equality of opportunity" is denied, and as this phrase is part of our holy of holies, then words that describe the doors through which pass the achievers must also be sacred. "Universalism" and "standardized examinations" are in truth distressingly neglected or rigged in caudillaje culture.

Yet for someone within caudillaje culture a very different interpretation emerges. According to the above statement at least five criteria are available for possible entrance to government service: (1) kinship; (2) membership in a certain club; (3) membership in a political faction; (4) friendship; (5) etc.

Except for number 1, these will depend upon one's aggregative skills. True, the first will often determine the level at which one begins, but certainly, once begun and skillfully played, the game has infinite possibilities. In fact, the public man will scan requirements for a position, and nothing will discourage him so much as a standardized examination. For many these exams, if rigidly adhered to, would mean the end of the road in terms of upward social mobility. Only the educated would have access to such jobs because education more than any other qualification demands affluence. Friendship, membership in a club or political faction, and those wonderful possibilities embodied in "etc." mean that everyman can perceive the probability of some success. Particularistic selection within the bureaucracy becomes in this sense as rational as universalism. That obvious truism prevents caudillaje society from adopting a merit system as we know it in other than name—they already have their own merit system. Anonymously graded competitive examinations make no sense where public power is the goal. Friends and relatives can contribute to that goal, but followership can hardly be tied to answering a civil service examination or doing geometry.

Examples of the unimportance of examinations for advancement in caudillaje society amplify the point. In his study of the Guatemalan bureaucracy Jerry Weaver found that "most Guatemalan bureaucrats see themselves being evaluated and promoted on the basis of criteria other than manifest skill, training, or experience. Only 20% of the sample thought that specific skills, technical training or on-the-job experience was most important for promotion." [96] Gavin Maxwell, in *The Ten Pains of Death*, interviews a "Dr. Spinato" who tells how he received his degree from Palermo University.

> I got my degree, but don't run away with the idea that it was due just to my sacrifices; on the contrary, I freely admit that if it hadn't been for the influence which my father exerted on the university bigwigs, I should certainly still be buried in my books at this very moment. It's not enough to work like a beaver at the university—even if I had worked, which I didn't—you need something else—power behind you. . . . I didn't bother to sit for examinations and so I dropped further and further behind. But there came a point when I realized that time was passing and that I was already twenty-seven. All things considered, it would take me two years to get my degree. Do you think I was going to put up with two years intense study? Most certainly not. But I had to get a degree, and anyway I wanted one. Only my father could manage to set the wheels of influence rolling. Fortunately for me, he's got friends everywhere, influential in every field of activity, even in politics.
>
> But I wanted to work in the certainty that I'd be passed whatever answers I gave. Before a university professor will pass you in a particular subject, he makes three conditions: either you know your subject inside out; or you've been well recommended; or you've paid him generously. In my case it was the last two conditions: recommendations and generous sums of money.[97]

Behavior may or may not accord with legal procedures of selection but tends to be extremely routinized. The public man depends upon his family and friends for access to position the way private capitalist men put faith in education as a vehicle for meeting entrance requirements to gain position. To believe that there is not a rational procedure for the acquiring of friends belies the facts, as we shall see in chapter 2. At times even family has been "created" where none existed. All of this requires enormous skill and competence albeit of a nontechnological, nonbureaucratic, noncapitalistic nature. In short, the procedure fails to be legal but passes the test for rationality.

Finally, while one would be foolish to downplay the importance of family within caudillaje society, still, the matter must be kept within perspective. Obviously, to be born to wealth anywhere in capitalistic culture means that one's life chances are significantly different from those who are not. Yet in some version the Horatio Alger myth remains a culture belief for capitalistic man even among the poor. One finds here the essence of the situation within caudillaje culture. Certain individuals begin much higher up on the scale of public influence than others, yet this does not guarantee them success or absolutely prohibit the rise of those born to parents who lack status: it simply means fewer obstacles for them to overcome.

The distinctions I have tried to draw between capitalistic and caudillaje cultures, between the public man and the private man, extend also into the area of criminality. René de Visme Williamson in his perceptive work, *Culture and Policy*, contrasts the North American gangster with the Hispanic world's "bandit" or "revolutionary":

The typical gangster is definitely not a Spaniard. He is an indigenous American type. For one thing, he is a businessman out to make money and engaged in activities that are prohibited by the law. Even the criterion of legality does not differentiate him perfectly from other businessmen, however, because the legality of "legitimate" business is sometimes the thinnest technicality and the animating spirit is generally the same. . . . The Spanish bandit, on the other hand, is much more likely to be a politician and could hardly be described as a businessman even though he might be taking in a good deal of money in the form of bribes or other illegally gotten income. His band is more in the nature of an association of free and equal men who cooperate with each other from choice in their common fight against society, and he is more

apt to ride on horseback openly than to drive a car behind drawn
shades under the cover of darkness.[98]

In short, bandits within the Hispanic world strive for public power,
while gangsters of the capitalistic world more directly pursue private
wealth. While each group may appear to be dysfunctional within their
larger community, still they operate within the value structure of their
respective cultures.

Setting also is in part determined by the spirit of caudillaje. While
one could easily claim too much here, urbanization in caudillaje culture
appears to stem in some measure from the individual's desire to surround himself. An urban setting contributes the most ideal conditions
for exercising a code of public virtue and the aggregation of friends.
One's extended family may suffice for a beginning, but ultimately one
must seek a broader constituency. Here lies a partial explanation for
the persistence with which caudillaje societies continue to urbanize
even when conditions in rural areas are improved: opportunity for
aggregating followers becomes greatly augmented within cities. This
helps explain why there are, for example, more cities of over 500,000
in Latin America than within the United States—over an area that in
terms of the usual industrialization-urbanization thesis should be the
reverse.[99] Although some delight in being a big fish in a very small
provincial pond, *preferirse ser cabeza de ratón, que cola de león* ("to
prefer to be the head of a mouse, than the tail of a lion"), most choose
the city with its unlimited human resources waiting to be tapped.
"Neighboring," or interaction between neighbors, naturally tends to
be higher in caudillaje urban areas than in capitalist cities and serves as
one of the attractions.[100] While capitalistic values drove nineteenth-
century poor to homestead the land in the United States, caudillaje
values assist the drive of twentieth-century poor to the cities throughout the Catholic world. As Jesús Sánchez says, "In the provinces a
child does not have the same opportunities children have in the capital." [101] Certainly no financial motive could adequately explain this
move to the urban areas. Indeed, many if not most are worse off economically in the cities than they were in the countryside.[102] One finds
support for that thesis in history. In Latin America when public men
had occasion to innovate in the creation of cities, economic considerations took second place. An indication of this truth resides in the fact
that "the political structure embodied in the act of foundation in Latin
America preceded the economic function." [103]

In short, the business of aggregation is taken seriously in caudillaje culture. While their counterparts in Protestant bourgeois culture are out selling newspapers, young people in these areas of the world—from Vienna to Buenos Aires—are already sitting in cafes beginning to accumulate their fortunes via the coinage system of public power. Here lies the unity of theory and practice. Caudillaje youth in their coffee-houses are not engaging in idle chatter. They are learning the criteria of public activity and beginning to apply their knowledge through the aggregation of friends, some of whom will be useful for a lifetime.

II

THE CATHOLIC ETHOS

Here I will try to demonstrate how becoming a public man necessarily involves one in the use of certain explicit, defined, and predictable behavior patterns. It will be shown that given the goal of public power these patterns or means are wholly rational. And finally, my aim is to establish the public nature of these behavior patterns. We thus will necessarily be discussing public virtue.

As shown above, in caudillaje culture everyman endeavors to be the public man. That is, he strives to practice in everyday life those virtues historically associated with public leadership. For it is through the practice of those virtues that public power is to be gained. Once value priorities become universally accepted within a society, rewards are dealt out within the merit framework established. One can see that public power does tend to be built upon actual possession and exhibition of these virtues. However, as will be shown, this does not have to be the case.

Given the life goal of public power, what kind of behavior might one anticipate within caudillaje society? How can men rationally act so as to achieve self-worth inside a culture that values the holding of power? Succinctly formulated, my thesis is that within those countries imbued with a spirit of caudillaje one finds an ethos which grants individual deference and respect on the basis of the taking and holding of public power; and the accepted mode for taking power resides in the ability to aggregate people through a code of public excellence. What is important for us here is the pervasiveness of caudillaje values among all social classes, the central function of aggregating friends, and the ethical code of behavior by which this aggregation is accomplished.

The behavior of the public man is patterned around a series of public or "aggregation" virtues. While everyman cannot be the holder of public power, everyman can endeavor to exercise those virtues associated with the public man. Thus, if one looks to caudillaje society he sees universally employed the virtues of public men: dignity, generosity, manliness, grandeur, and leisure. It is these that are utilized for the aggregation of persons. Caudillaje relationships are, in short, permeated with public virtues, publicly displayed.

One sees a public form of excellence everywhere attempted within caudillaje countries. For example, the home—that most private of institutions—must have its public "front." Living rooms will often be magnificently furnished while bathrooms, kitchens, and other more "private" facilities may exist in a decrepit state. In more recent times it is not unusual to find a new refrigerator or other appliance displayed in the lower-middle-class front room to publicly signify one's worth. The Protestant-capitalist tradition, by contrast, is more uniform. Public and private are more intermingled. One's public side tends to reflect the same coarseness or grandeur as his private side. Grant Wood portraits attest to the simple life believed pleasing to God by these privately oriented people. The kitchen and the parlor are equal.

Let us review some of these aggregating or public virtues. Consider leisure. For a citizen of a Protestant-ethic country, it is perhaps difficult to think of leisure as a virtue because all one's life he has heard of the virtue of activity; because, as Luther said, "he cannot ever in this life be idle." [1] Leisure he considers merely as the absence of work, and if he is over fifty years old he probably knows that "idle hands are the tools of the devil." Thereby leisure is given a negative connotation. In general, capitalist-industrial society has viewed leisure unfavorably because it is not useful, it does not produce anything. Hence, Protestant-ethic man endeavors to turn his spare time, vacations, retirement, sabbatical year, into work. It was Ben Franklin who defined leisure as a "time for doing something useful." [2] Therefore, one must take courses in the university, learn "how to" build his own boat, "take up" reading, etc., etc.

Caudillaje man, by contrast, actively and rationally utilizes leisure for the advancement of his goal of public power. ("To be a professor in this country [Uruguay] is a hobby, a hobby one engages in for prestige.")[3] While capitalist man uses his time off to *produce* goods, caudillaje man uses his nonworking hours to *aggregate* persons. And in his use of leisure this public man exhibits a marked degree of rationality. For example, leisure to be useful must be observed by others.

The man of public power obviously is a person who cannot be bothered by trifles such as the clock. Therefore, like kings of old, he arrives when he arrives. Much of this is implicit in the example given at the beginning of chapter 1. When a person of power makes his grand entrance, his retainers should be waiting and events may only then proceed. And for all of this there must be behavioral norms: "Half past ten [is] rather early to appear at a ball if one is Prince of Salina." [4] Thus the habit of keeping late hours in caudillaje societies can be easily justified as rational behavior, just as the capitalist, early-to-bed-early-to-rise philosophy is consistent with a production ethic. V. S. Pritchett in *Dublin* condenses the behavioral differences between a cultural ethos of *el grand señor* and that of the private capitalist: "Keeping late hours . . . is a secondary religious characteristic. If a man goes to bed late, he is a Catholic; if he goes early he is a Protestant." [5]

The outward leisurely pace of caudillaje life is deceptive. Private business has often languished because men were pursuing their public business (that is, the game of public power) with an assiduousness and aggressiveness that would do credit to a North American salesman. Of course, the rules are different, but the amount of time and nervous energy which caudillaje man devotes to his public image are absolutely enormous.

I am reminded, for example, of a very aggressive and politically ambitious Latin American friend of mine. On more than one occasion I have been invited to go with him to keep an appointment with a North American. Long before the appointed time he is ready and pacing the floor looking at his watch. At a suitably tardy moment he decides to go and we race off in his chauffeur-driven car. We arrive, he excuses himself for having been delayed by other matters. His public worth thus having been established, we get down to business. The North Americans curse to themselves about the way he disregards time. In reality they are saying that self-interest should compel him to arrive at the appointed hour.[6] My Latin American friend, by contrast, has just seen the triumph of public virtue. All were waiting, the king has arrived, long live the king!

The ethos of Protestantism proclaimed an importance bordering on the sacred for time. For Protestant man "loss of time through sociability, idle talk, luxury" was, as Max Weber pointed out, "worthy of absolute moral condemnation." [7] Ben Franklin, spokesman for the ethos, had insisted, "time is money," and time must therefore be saved, utilized, and spent wisely. Now caudillaje man knows that "time brings with it all things, and may produce indifferently either good or evil." [8] He intuits that time is important only in the sense that power can be acquired or lost through his utilization of it. Yet he behaves in a totally rational fashion when, for example, he spends hours in cafes talking to his friends. For here is the source of his power, the sine qua non of his existence. Without spending time in this fashion he would, in fact, soon have fewer friends. Additionally, he knows that to leave a cafe precipitously for an "appointment" would signify to all that he must not keep someone else waiting—which further indicates his lack of importance. If he had power and position the other person would wait upon his arrival. It is the powerless who wait. He also runs the danger of offending those whom he is with by his desire to leave, showing a lack of esteem for present company. Given these considerations, the often heard Spanish toast, *salud, amor, pesetas y tiempo para gozarlos* ("health, love, money, and time to enjoy them"), takes on added meaning. Such an adage shows not merely a wish preference, but derives from and reflects a rational world view. Caudillaje society, unlike that of capitalism, logically then embraces a more here-and-now attitude. "Time to enjoy" reinforces the public-man ethos of caudillaje culture in much the same way that "time is money" supports the private-man ethos of capitalism. For example, Italians quite obviously do not believe that time is money. Witness their communications media. Television programs are not any particular length. "Instead of a program, whether on film or transmitted live, being planned to fit a predesignated time period, the time period, logically enough, is adjusted to accommodate the program." [9] Over the years this attitude toward time has become part of the social mores of Catholic countries. Brendan Behan characterized the Irish disposition in this regard by titling one of his books *Hold Your Hour and Have Another*. [10]

There is an additional side to this studied neglect of time: the premise that a great man, a public man, presumably would have such weighty business to attend to that he could not possibly adhere to a schedule. The student described at the beginning of this work once arrived at my house for a 9:00 P.M. dinner-party invitation at 11:15 P.M. Obviously, in this case the implication was that he had such important matters to attend to that an earlier time would have been inconceivable —as would a telephone call to inform his host of the delay. Similar behavior in everyday life is also displayed on the national level by political leaders of whatever persuasion. Both Juan Perón and Fidel Castro, among others, have practiced the art of interminable delay before appearing to give speeches before the thousands. It seems, in fact, to effectively build enthusiasm among the hearers. In short, social-political functions and private appointments in Catholic culture invariably begin late to allow for the individual's demonstration of excellence. But one should ever bear in mind that the concept "late" can only be applied by someone from outside the ethos. Culture is rooted in shared expectations. It is the foreigner who arrives "on time" who has acted irrationally and without grace—disrupting the harmony of a consistently functioning ethos.

Leisure in caudillaje society provides a positive referent for the public man as does work for capitalistic societies. There exists widespread authority for this statement. Lawrence Suhm writes, "It would ... be no exaggeration to say that leisure and leisure occupations are as important to the Latin Americans as work and work occupations are to the North Amerians." William Stokes sums up a larger cultural area by stating that "Hispanic culture has long been characterized by the belief that leisure ennobles and labor, especially technical labor, degrades." Referring to the debasing quality of work, a study of Poland states: "Its children have cultivated the earth and cultivated their minds for centuries, but they have at the same time obstinately regarded work merely for money as a low, degrading thing. They have nourished the inherited aristocratic contempt for the merchant and the manufacturer, to say nothing of the shopkeeper and the mechanic. They have collected great fortunes, but they have spent them. Money was a means; very seldom an end: work a semi-disgraceful resource; never its own reward." Kurt Karfield writes, "more perhaps than any European people since the Ancients, the Austrian still tries to build his real life around his leisure hours." [11]

Differences of the two perspectives have been lucidly brought to attention where Protestant missionaries have sought a following in Latin America. Emilio Willems reports that "most converts found it strange that otiosity, irregular and undisciplined working methods, and leisure should be attacked as sinful." [12] The unity of Christianity and routinized activity lacks a self-evident quality. Only when Protestantism became codified was the equation tenable to the West.

One can additionally perceive the difference by comparing life on a large caudillaje farm with existence on a big capitalistic farm. In the first instance activity is usually organized not so much to maximize production as to maintain and perpetuate itself. The owner comes to his land to enjoy himself, and squeezing every penny from the land is hardly part of that plan. In Jorge Icaza's story of *Huasipungo*, Don Alfonso typifies this attitude in overstated form: he believed it something unheard of for a master to get up at midnight just to save his crops from the cows that had gotten into the cornfield.[13] Samuel Shapiro writes:

> Even educated Latin Americans seem to lack drive and entrepreneurial skill required to build an industrial civilization. The badly-managed and unproductive *hacienda* provides for its owner a comfortable way of life, with few worries, much leisure, and an abundance of cheap household help. He derives from it some cash income, which he is likely to invest in urban real estate—or in Wall Street or Switzerland—and he is definitely not interested in becoming a rival to some North American millionaire. When American captains of industry like Rockefeller, Carnegie, and Ford made money, they reinvested it and set about making more, a process that led to mass production, economy of scale and huge industries. For the South American, on the other hand, business has never been an end in itself, but only a way to get enough money to enjoy life. . . .
>
> As a consequence of this psychological attitude, and recurrent political instability that makes it impossible to plan for the long future, few businessmen in Argentina or Chile drive themselves in the manner of a nineteenth century American captain of industry or a contemporary "Organization Man." The ideal is to accumulate a fortune, preferably in farm land or city apartments that can be handled by a manager, large enough to live on comfortably. The aim of life is the intelligent enjoyment of leisure.[14]

Another author, discussing Brazilian history, says:

When the optimism and the confidence of the first hours of independence were over, when the Brazilian was still fascinated with the drugs, minerals, grandeur, and power . . . he choked off his feeling of insufficiency with an endless catalog of his riches— which were not so readily come by as he had previously thought —and as a result of his own natural tendencies he became unrealistic. This is what lies at the root of Brazilian nationalist boasting— riches, not tasks to be performed; excellencies, rather than economic and spiritual sufficiencies.

It was not recognized that the great sin was poverty, which

could be overcome by work and saving. Work was scorned; it was reserved exclusively for slaves. No attention was paid to saving, with the result that the capital required for possession and enjoyment of the riches so greatly vaunted in speeches was never accumulated.[15]

Such attitudes in both their historic and contemporary forms are wholly rational from the public-man point of view. Caudillaje man, no doubt with images of Cicero in his head, performs as a man of consequence. Like the public men of Greece and Rome, his existence is supported by those lower in socioeconomic class. Endeavoring to maximize profits would actually lower the status of the *patrón*[16] because it would demonstrate that, like the *campesinos*, he has to take care, to save, and finally to work in order to provide for tomorrow. To the extent that this is in fact necessary for him, he appoints a manager. But the manager's foremost task is to supply a buffer between work and leisure, between the public man and inferiors. It is this intermediary position which allows the *patrón* to play both the benefactor of the *campesinos* in a direct role—as a public man is by definition charitable—and simultaneously their exploiter through the medium of his manager.

Capitalistic farms offer no buffers between exploitation and charity. The owner traditionally works with the hired help, and both are dehumanized by the mechanization now achieved. No doubt this results because the machine accentuates what was always inherent in capitalist endeavor, the equation of time and money on the one hand and competition between owner and worker on the other. Whether realized in an Iowa cornfield or according to the Marxist dialectical thesis of bourgeoisie and its antithesis in the proletariat, the conclusion is the same: work is both necessary and good because of its tie to production.

Caudillaje society does not glorify production per se. (The villager Pancrazio "had recognized early that neither the land nor manual labor offered a future with respect. A living, yes, but not respect.")[17] Consequently, the virtues upon which production depends are not viable within that culture any more than they were relevant to life in ancient Greece or Rome. The public-man image demands free time for its fulfillment. Phrases supporting a leisure-oriented world view abound in caudillaje society. None better demonstrates this than the catchy Brazilian saying that *o ocio vale mais do que lo negocio* ("leisure is better than occupation"). Behavioral and economic implications of the leisure-oriented society can be imagined by considering Robert Theobald's words: "If an individual prefers leisure to work, it is perfectly rational that he would do as little work as possible. Any attempt to deal with a shortage of workers in this situation by raising wages—a rational action in the rich countries—might aggravate the problem under these circumstances." [18] My point here consists in emphasizing that a positive attitude toward leisure by definition makes an overemphasis upon work a nonrational attitude. And caudillaje culture has been wholly rational, given its public-man goals, in deprecating the value of work. That this attitude is not mere whimsy upon the part of random individuals but a culturewide value becomes evident. *Ariel*, one of the most widely read works in Latin American literature, in defining leisure illustrates the ideal. "To think, to dream, to admire—these are the ministrants that haunt my cell. The ancients ranked them under the word *otium*, well-employed leisure, which they deemed the highest use of being truly rational; liberty of thought emancipated of all ignoble chains. Such leisure meant that use of time which they opposed to mere economic activity as the expression of a higher life. Their concept of dignity was linked closely to this lofty conception of leisure." [19] It follows that not Canada or the United States but Uruguay was the first nation in this hemisphere to establish a limit upon work in the form of an eight-hour-day and a forty-eight-hour-week. Interestingly, this movement for limiting the hours of labor in caudillaje culture appears not to have evolved through pressure from the working class, as occurred in capitalistic societies. Rather, intellectuals seem to have taken up the theme out of a belief that all work was an evil to be avoided as far as possible. For example, one of those influential in establishing limits upon work in Uruguay, Domingo Arena, a senator during the presidency of Batlle wrote, "He who works, then, is always subjected, whatever the nature of his work might be." [20] The task of a sales clerk may well be as onerous as that of a steel worker seen from the public-man perspective. Arena's comment sounds somewhat Marxist. That Marxism as a theory has found such a favorable reception throughout caudillaje lands, is due, I believe, in no small part to its strong condemnation of the exploitation of the working class. Naturally, to a culture that sees limited utility in work, such a theory is prima facie good.[21] At base, however, caudillaje values are oriented more toward eliminating work than toward abolishing exploitation. As Castro has found to his chagrin, Cubans tend to define all work as exploitation, an imposition, something to be avoided.

The moral attitudes of caudillaje man are colored with utilitarianism. Public virtues such as grandeur, generosity, and manliness are useful *because* they help in the aggregation of followers and it is this which makes them virtues.[22] One can also see that fact illuminated in the matter of leisure and work. Caudillaje society's posture toward physical labor exemplifies an aspect of this highly consistent and pragmatic value system. A public man might fight battles, administer estates, run a government, but surely he would not stoop to physical labor. Levine in *Main Street Italy* notes that "especially when a man is a doctor—a *dottore*—he must behave in a certain way out of his house even if he is not capable of earning a living. Some people think a man with a university degree should never go to the market to buy a kilogram of tomatoes; especially in the south an educated man will seldom carry a package home." [23] Lowry Nelson wrote of Cuba: "The upper-class Cuban husband assumes very few of the menial responsibilities which are almost universally accepted by his counterpart in the United States. For example, he would not expect to fix a leaky water-tap, or repair light switches, mow the lawn, look after the garden, and certainly not to wash his own automobile. These are the tasks for the *chofer* and the gardener and the poor boy who seeks to earn a few pennies for clearing out the garage. They are tasks reserved for the lower class." [24] But those qualities similarly characterize the lower classes in their actions and orientations toward the world. For example, a restaurateur in Spain says, a man "won't pick up a broom or help his wife wash up. Never! The trouble we had getting our waiter to sweep the floor. He was scared out of his life someone would see him with a broom in his hand and laugh at him for being a woman. Each time someone passed he'd hide the broom!" [25] Richard Adams in an essay, "Rural Labor," summarizes research on attitudes toward physical labor in some rural caudillaje societies: "Indeed, there is little evidence that the rural worker (either independent or wage-earner) is singly devoted to work. In studies of Puerto Rico, Mexico, Colombia, Peru, Paraguay, and Brazil, the story is the same, differing only in emphasis. The most positive attitude reported is that of the Canamelar worker: 'He will be ... hardworking, but not to the extent that it interferes with his social obligations.' The most exaggerated attitude is that reported from the Colombian town of Aritama, where ... work is openly despised and even the implication that one is engaging in it is regarded as an insult." [26] Such behavior has nothing to do with laziness or inertia but rather with a means/end formula. He who labors

with his hands will seldom be invited to associate with those who do
not. To rake one's own yard, wait on one's own table, wash one's own
car would be looked on askance by middle-class neighbors. Such activity might elicit paternal charity but never respect. Parsimony in
these matters can have no rewards in a society which celebrates the
public man. And those of the lower class who must wait on tables, wash
cars, and do gardening for a living can help to gain back a measure of
self-respect by having their own shoes shined by someone else, buying
a drink for a friend, giving a young peasant girl room and board to
wait on their table, or concealing their occupation by wearing a tie to
and from work.

Activity other than physical labor, however, does not carry an
especially negative connotation in caudillaje culture. From Italy come
the famous words of a dying father to his children: "My sons, you
must all try to have an occupation in life. Life without an occupation is
contemptible and meaningless. But always remember this: You must
never allow your occupation to degenerate into work." [27] Thus, like
leisure for capitalistic man, one's occupation must be useful. But utility
is in this case tied to a goal of public power. As Machiavelli, the most
famous exponent of this position, stated the matter for those in authority: "A wise prince should . . . never remain idle in peaceful times, but
industriously make good use of them, so that when fortune changes she
may find him prepared to resist her blows." [28] Translated into caudillaje
social terms, this means that activity must be steady and directed—but
not necessarily oriented toward economic productivity.

Another public virtue is that of grandeur. Grandeur more than
anything else establishes what an Irish Catholic writer, Ulick O'Connor,
has called "an aristocracy of personality." [29] Used in the broad sense,
we are speaking of an image of individual excellence embodying magnificence which can be displayed in a public forum. For example, an
author asserts that "only in Vienna may one rise from a seat in a
theater, carefully adjust his opera glasses and deliberately scan the
whole audience as if searching for a friend or enemy. No matter where
your seat is located you may enjoy such a 'rubber' to your heart's
content. Naturally the pleasure derived from such a performance is
largely proportional to the quality of your attire." [30] This perceptive
author errs in believing that such display-type behavior only exists in
Austria. It characterizes other Catholic countries as well. The criterion
of illustriousness tends to be embodied in actions useful for the acquisition of public power. Machado de Assis, a Brazilian, cleverly portrayed

numerous facets to the care and feeding of public grandeur in his short story, "Education of a Stuffed Shirt." Publicity, he said, "is an imperious and demanding mistress that you must woo with a host of little trinkets, comfits, cushions for her back, trifling attentions that betoken the constancy of your affection rather than the boldness and ambition of your desire." [31] Machado then proceeds to detail various acts one may perform to achieve such humbly inspired publicity. The important thing is to place one's name before the world. To accomplish this feat one needs to have portraits available for display—if pressed by friends—newspaper reporters about, and a gift for oratory. Such a combination is foolproof!

Grandeur is perhaps most notably displayed through oratorical ability, a developed art form throughout caudillaje culture. Oratory has nothing to do with either scientific demonstration or empirical reality, but with convincing others of the correctness of one's position. A great many of the men who have risen to power in modern caudillaje polities have had significant speaking ability. By way of illustration consider the Argentine gaucho leader, Juan Manuel Rosas, who has been characterized as "a vehement and passionate orator";[32] or the Ecuadorian José María Velasco Ibarra's famous boast—confirmed by his return to the presidency five times—"Give me a balcony and the people are mine"; or Benito Mussolini, Italian dictator of the 1930s and forties, who has been described as "one of the best and most moving speakers in Italy," [33] which should come as no surprise in a right-wing caudillaje polity of that time. Similarly, it has been said of a left-wing dictator in a contemporary caudillaje polity that even in university days "students were a little in awe of Fidel. His remarkable ability at oratory usually resulted in the students giving him his way without opposition." [34] Oratorical skill smoothes the way to power. In Mariano Azuela's *Los de abajo*, readers are treated to an example of the founding of a leader-follower relationship based upon oral skill. The characters are stretched out on rocks listening to Venancio, the barber and medicine man, skillfully recount some episodes from *The Wandering Jew*, after which Luis Cervantes speaks:

"Admirable! You have a remarkable talent!"

"I'm not so bad," said the self-assured Venancio, "but my parents died and I wasn't able to study for a career."

"That's no hindrance. Two or three weeks of assisting at a hospital, a good recommendation from our chief Macias and you're a doctor. You have such an aptitude that it will be child's play."

After that night, Venancio differed from the rest, for he no longer called him "curro." It was "Luisito" here and "Luisito" there.[35]

Elocution in a caudillaje setting constitutes a much more compelling media than does mere wealth. "In Spain," says Michener, "words form a kind of currency which must be spent freely." [36] One should hardly be startled, therefore, to see this skill exhibited extensively. Thus, an Irishman heads for the pub "not so much because he wants a drink but mainly because he wants to talk before an audience. That's the Irish pub, a stage for the orator, and that's an Irishman—a performer who loves to hear himself talk." [37] Embellishments will be welcome. Haven't all public men adorned their speech? In Edwin Cerio's *Aria di Capri*, the mayor, Costanziello Veruotto, has decided to learn a few well-chosen Latin words—essential to political speeches—from the priest. "The Canon himself considered that speeches without Latin were like loaves without leaven; they all fell flat." [38] Thus, the "tone" of the mayor's discourse would be improved.

Few persons in caudillaje society are unwilling or unable to speak extemporaneously on almost any subject. To say that such speeches are "uninformed" would be to miss the point, for it is not content but style that is appreciated by one's listener. Does he "sound" like a public man is the question. As Consuelo Sánchez said of the Mexican male, "he is not interested in learning the truth, but only in out-talking the others." [39]

A personal digression illustrates the value of speaking style over content. Some years ago I began teaching in Latin America at the graduate level. My first class was memorable. After outlining the course plan for students, I belatedly thought to find out just how advanced they were by asking some informational questions. The first question: "Do you understand the concept of 'faction' as used by Simón Bolívar?" There was only the slightest of pauses before a young man's hand went up. I recognized him. Whereupon he stood, cleared his throat, squared his shoulders, buttoned his coat, and began a twenty-five minute discourse on the glories of Bolívar: the profundities of his thought, the factions against which he had fought so gloriously, etc., etc. While it was quite obvious—to me—that he had no idea at all of Bolívar's specific writings, speeches, or ideas on politics, this orator did know what a faction was, he did know who Bolívar was, he did know about the Godos, creoles, and the war with Spain. He therefore put them all together and gave a moving, impassioned call for a return to the ideals of the *Libertador* building up to a crescendo with a plea for the freedom of his own *patria* from the demagogues who were ruining it. Students wildly applauded when he finished. Grandeur again triumphed over facts. Totally disoriented, I dismissed the class and, holding tightly to a copy of the *Selected Writings of Bolívar*, made my way to the bar at the American Club.

A retired Sicilian doctor recalls an anecdote about a *festa* which underscores the importance of presentation over substance rather nicely. (Only those readers from capitalist cultures will ask about the veracity of the tale!)

> We've got a good story here in Sicily about one of the deputies engaging a preacher for this last sermon. The deputy had found a preacher, nice black beard and flashing eyes and all, and they got down to discussing terms.
>
> "May I ask, Father," said the deputy, "what remuneration you would require to preach this sermon?"
>
> "Well, my son," said the friar, "I've got a very nice sermon that everybody would understand, at 20,000 lire."
>
> "And have you any better than that one, Father?"
>
> "Well, there's one at 50,000 lire, which the educated people would understand."
>
> "And anything better still, Father?"
>
> "Yes, indeed: there's one at 75,000 lire which only the priest and the mayor and the deputies and I would understand.
>
> "Any *still* better, Father?"
>
> "Yes—for 100,000 lire, I preach one that only the priest and I will understand."
>
> "We have money to spend this year, Father; is there yet another sermon?"
>
> "There is, my son—for 150,000 lire I preach a sermon which I don't understand a single word of myself!"
>
> "Then," said the deputy, "we will settle on that one, Father." [40]

One must keep in mind that grandeur is useful to a public man while facts very often are not.[41] In judicial matters, for instance, decisions tend to reflect even more the oratorical facility of the participants than is the case in capitalist polities. Witnesses, for example, often see the court as "something between a stage and an arena," where one comes "prepared to do battle with every weapon at his disposal, even one as insidious as the truth." [42] When one speaks of grandeur as a virtue the implication is that society will reward a variety of public skills. In fact, grandeur can refer to any type of excellence that may be publicly displayed. Stendhal in "The Abbess of Castro," a story about sixteenth-century Italy, captured this attitude. "In Italy," he said, "a man distinguished himself by all forms of merit, by famous strokes with the sword as by discoveries in ancient manuscripts: take Petrarch, the idol of his time; and a women of the sixteenth century loved a man who was learned in Greek as well as, if not more than, she would have loved a man famous for his martial valour." [43] What Stendhal meant is that special excellence when publicly displayed will be commended.[44] Certainly the virtues of grandeur require more than a knowledge of Greek or becoming a writer: a writer can publicly distribute books to his friends and dedicate them to persons of power (as Machiavelli did and is still done in caudillaje culture today); while the habit of oratory allows a public display of one's knowledge of Greek phrases—even in coffeehouses. Such activity gives an entirely different dimension to formal learning than is associated with knowledge in Protestant countries. It is not the "truth" per se that sets caudillaje man free but the manner in which information is presented and conveyed which establishes its veracity. Fidel Castro, for example, can captivate a standing audience of tens of thousands for four to six hours. Yet the majority of persons appear to have only the vaguest idea of his reasoning and subtleties. An Italian journalist in addressing himself to this phenomenon in the press said: "Call it lack of principle if you want to, but it's not part of the *ambiente* [atmosphere]. It's in the Italian character. Italians are not educated to a conscious search for fact. Mussolini was all bluff and this contributed too. Catholic education stresses trusting in the future, not seeking facts. The Catholic Church preaches that certain things should be repressed. This suits the parties which suppress news for their own purposes. In fact, our very language lends itself to the substitution of opinion for facts." [45] Here lies one of the reasons that the public man prefers the "academic" over the "applied" disciplines in the university. In the former he has the opportunity to exhibit his virtues while still in the university and also prepare himself for a life of public activity. Engineering, agriculture, physics, and so on, offer no such opportunities for development in this direction,[46] and neither do such typically Protestant-ethic university majors as sociology, political science, and anthropology. These have also been traditionally avoided in caudillaje higher education. (As those subjects have become more imbued with formalistic scholasticism of the behavioral persuasion, they have begun to "catch on" in caudillaje culture.) The importance of architecture in the curriculum, by contrast, demonstrates the point. Caudillaje areas of the world are all graced with great cathedrals and magnificient public buildings. From the splendid and daring design and execution of modern Brasília backward through the Renaissance to the Middle Ages this has been so. One can see that the developed study of architecture within caudillaje societies and the many students entering the field confirm my thesis—that architecture is a wholly public profession. One's work or "product," however insignificant, becomes a public monument to its designer. Internal plumbing, elevators, crumbling plaster, and upkeep in general are more private and thus tend to be neglected. What counts is not so much a job "well done" as a job "well applauded."

Like students, professors pursue university life for its obvious public opportunities. Prestige and respect—these are their goals. Although his university salary is usually insignificant and uncertain, caudillaje man covets a teaching position because it can be useful in his quest for public power. "With his name, title, connections, civil service status and life-long position ensured, he is often tempted to use his chair as a mere rung on the long social climb to power. Once made 'catedrático' [professor], he no longer has to worry much about teaching and less about research. Aided and sustained by his university post, he is at last free to launch upon a successful professional or even political career." [47]

"Philosophic" grandeur hinges on its utility in the proclamation of authoritative comments upon a large realm of subjects. Naturally a public man may never err upon any subject—his wisdom reigns absolute. Therefore, he will gravitate almost inevitably to a form of discourse filled with a margin of ambiguity. What could be more ready-made for this purpose than topics pertaining to law, philosophy, literature, politics, and religion? One sees continually the phenomenon of men discussing these matters in absolutist terms. No faltering is allowed for the public man. For example, a schoolmaster complaining of difficult matters such as the existence of God and the meaning of happiness grants that there are "embarrassing questions that one can't explain in a few words, but I have to satisfy their [students] demands even if I make mistakes in doing so—if I said I didn't know I'd be ruined." [48] Or the typical example of a priest who sums up his inadequate responses to villagers' questions: "And I have to answer all these questions, and sometimes I'm at a loss, but if I didn't answer I'd cut a sorry figure—for better or worse I've got to answer." [49] Such explicit and often wrong answers have become part of the landscape of caudillaje culture. The grandeur of a public man, whether giving directions to a place he's never heard of or discussing international events about which he is largely uninformed, depends upon his providing definite, incontrovertible information. Of course, those who live in caudillaje society are quite aware that much of what is said contains error, bombast, and fiction. Rarely, however, do they challenge such authority directly. To do so would open a state of war and question the integrity of the speaker. And toward what end? One probably did not listen to him in the first place for information but because of his place and station within the society, or due to the possibility of including the speaker in one's circle of friends.

Learning thus has a public utility in caudillaje countries. Education is geared to play a supportive role in an individual's aspiration for public power. Public virtue cannot be found in private meditation of the monastery or chapel, nor is the worldly asceticism of Protestantism likely to assist in the development of one's needed virtues. Rather, virtue of this type can only be acquired in the public forum. What one learns, in secularized form, are those lessons of public behavior taught by the scholastics, by Machiavelli, by Bolívar and other great mentors of their tradition.

Public virtue can be attained through the Aristotelian mode of practice. Habit is essential.[50] But virtue can only be developed through education, through the inculcation of the values of the public man. Universities from medieval times to the very recent past were entirely geared toward the professions. That is, caudillaje students were learning something that would be useful. And clearly what is useful centers not so much on content as upon the public presentation of a matter. Facts are private, book reading is private, research is private. These depend upon personal initiative—and who can say what a person has privately learned? Hence those pursuits tend to be neglected by caudillaje man, the reward for such academic enterprise being essentially internal rather than public. Activities which can be socially rewarding constitute the focus of his education and later years. A Guatemalan novelist captures admirably the essence of this ethos. One of his characters asserts: "You'll kill yourself or go crazy with all this studying! I've told you so from the first! Can't you understand that it's tact rather than knowledge you need if you want to get on?"[51] Caudillaje students who become technically proficient through some specialized study in the United States, England, or Scandinavia are often chagrined to find when they return home that less well-trained persons will usually be their superiors. While Juan was in the United States becoming "privately superior," Pedro was practicing the political art at home. In Latin America one observes the use of North American degrees as a claim to high position within the public realm. But there operates here a very subtle process. One has the feeling that the claim is advanced on the same level as another might assert his rights on the basis of having led a barracks revolt or having been exiled for ten years. It is somehow a heroic act to have gone among the barbarians of the North and pulled a "coup" by getting the degree. Such a coup, upon one's return to civilization, must be given public status!

Thus, education is even more assiduously sought in Latin America than in the United States because titles, degrees, diplomas have become even more useful there. They contribute to one's external presentation of self in giving the "appearance" of the cultivated man. Simón Bolívar, spokesman for the ethos, was, for example, insistent that "instruction should be given in manners and in the ceremonies and deference to be accorded all persons, in keeping with their stations." [52] Titles and degrees help identify and enhance "station." The appellation of "doctor" carried by everyone with a bachelor's degree exemplifies that reality.

Living one's rank forms an aspect of grandeur. Public men must live as public men—any other life style would call into question their worth as individuals. To mount solely an economic criterion for one's life style constitutes not only unseemly behavior but also, and more importantly, a confusion of value priorities. As Wagley points out, "labor and political leaders may lead luxurious and expensive lives in full view of their constituents. Latin Americans expect their leaders to live and behave in a manner befitting upper-class gentlemen." [53] In Protestant-ethic countries labor and political leaders may similarly lead lives of luxury signifying economic success—but never will they be allowed to take on the role, airs, or accent of a "gentleman" if their origins are in the middle or lower ranks of society. A façade of the "new man" brings scorn and derision.

Finally, grandeur indicates prowess, superior ability and/or position. While evocative of an elite, it is open to everyone. In writing of contemporary France, Jesse Pitts, mirroring the comments above on Italy by Stendhal, says, "prowess can be found at all levels. The creation of a piece of jewelry by a Parisian craftsman, the peasant's careful distillation of a liqueur, the civilian's stoicism in the face of Gestapo torture, Marcel Proust's suave gallantry in the salon of Madame de

Guermantes—all are examples of prowess in modern France." [54] This writer correctly stresses the need for the author of a special act or work to seduce the spectator. He must win approval for his accomplishment from others. His act becomes validated in his own eyes at the moment that "the spectator to it acknowledges the irresistible appeal of both the man and the deed" [55] Such heroics are daily performed at every social and economic level in caudillaje society.

Another public virtue is that of generosity. To a capitalist, generosity can easily spill over into frivolity because in the economic sense it risks the depletion of capital—he settles for tax-deductible gifts. For caudillaje man, however, generosity augments friendship. In other words, it builds his capital investment in the future. Rationally, then, he saves so that he can achieve a dazzling impact with the release of his capital. "Money is put away to be used on public occasions, to make a show." [56]

Contrary to life within the Protestant ethos, a lack of generosity can have nothing to do with self-denial. The public man does not feel called to give up wine, women, or song for some economic goal. Abstinence finds few imitators in that culture. On the level of social welfare, caudillaje persons appear to feel little need to quietly deny themselves any pleasures of life so that anonymous others may eat better. That kind of virtue is a particularly passive one of pietistic Protestant origins.[57] By contrast, a caudillaje individual wants to actively intervene in the cause of justice—he wants to *use* his virtue. Denial for him is a private act which he associates with his religion. Fasting or Lenten abstinence affects only his own salvation. But paying taxes, for example, is a form of forced private self-denial without religious or familial goals. This makes no sense to him as it does not lead to a positive public result. Others cannot know of his virtue if he honestly (and privately) pays his taxes.

In Catholic countries one sees grandiose public eleemosynary projects and niggardly private giving—magnificent buildings with the name of the benefactor prominently displayed upon the façade with no endowment for upkeep. One finds the same phenomena in the matter of private charity. Benevolence in caudillaje countries tends to be public —both the receiver and observer are thus made aware of the giver's largess. Thus, Lowry Nelson speaks of the First Lady in Cuba giving presents to the poor at Christmas time and comments, "The point is not that gifts are given to the poor—an act that is done in most countries— but solely in the manner of public giving." [58] Anonymous donations to community chests, regular support of the Church, or significant contributions to the Red Cross are rare in caudillaje society even among the well-to-do. For example, Desbarats writing about Catholic Quebec comments, "The Anglostocracy supports culture for the masses in a manner out of all proportion to its numerical strength in the city. It is difficult to think of large city-wide cultural institutions which are supported primarily by the French-Canadians on a voluntary basis. This sort of philanthropy is an Anglo-Saxon custom." [59] Yet traditionally before one dies it is not unusual to will much of one's estate to the Church, a school, or a city in order to build a cathedral, gymnasium, or statue. The reason may be that (1) this act has the merit of being public and thus satisfying the worldly ethic of public virtue, and (2) it may help to buy private salvation—and thus also satisfy the otherworldly ethic.[60] Of course, the paying of taxes could fulfill neither criteria.

Dignity is yet another caudillaje virtue. It becomes rational for the public man to be preoccupied over his dignity once one remembers that "rank" is a synonym for dignity. To worry about rank has always been the preoccupation of public men. Caudillaje society has made such concern both rational and culturewide. Dignity thus becomes an achievement virtue. If leisure embodies the goal of caudillaje men, it is a leisure built upon the attainment of dignity. In this they hark back to the Stoic-Greek influence of Cicero who asked, In what consists the goal set before these governors of the commonwealth? His answer: "It is leisure accompanied by dignity (cum dignitate otium)." [61] One must ever strive to rise in society, because dignity comes much easier to those at the top. Artemio Cruz, the protagonist of a well-known novel by Carlos Fuentes, despised what he termed the "chickenshit middleclass" built on the humbler virtues because it was bereft of dignity. "Yes," he says, "let them imagine that they belong to the world that is empty of my pride and decisions, the world they would know if I were virtuous and humble: down in that world that I know and have risen from. Or up here where I am now: only here, I tell them is dignity possible, not below in the middle of envy and monotony and standing in lines." [62]

For the public man, to lose his dignity is to be destroyed. He will readily sacrifice even his freedom in order to maintain this dignity.[63] Perhaps a parallel would be for a capitalist to lose his wealth. In both cases the sense of self-worth is at stake because one's peer group will indicate varying degrees of disapproval.[64] Consequently, in caudillaje society everyone will claim dignity even though he may feel he possesses very little.[65] Behaviorally, he will endeavor to live up to his image of such a person. Requisites pertaining to a man of dignified countenance and habits will be exacted from his fellowman—and if not forthcoming he will live in a state of private melancholy alternated with public desperation. "His chief care," as one Spanish author writes, "is *quedar proper*—to remain proper—to abide by the prescribed attitude. By 're-maining proper' a man earns his self-esteem. He shows that he can rise above circumstances. To 'remain proper' is one form of affirmation of the 'self.' " [66] One finds the same emphasis upon dignified behavior ob-served by all classes in Polish society. Poles reportedly take great pains to maintain their own dignity while also respecting that of others. "To be lacking in formality, politeness, and dignity is to be crude and to offend another person's honor.... Self-respect demands a display of good manners; little courtesies dot all of life. It is believed that each person one deals with should be made to feel that he is respected as an individual."[67]

Dignity is based upon reciprocity. One must be ever giving and getting. He who omits to give "proper" respect will be scorned and ostracized. He is failing to "pay his way" in the currency of caudillaje culture.

Too much, I think, has been written about the relationship of "soul" and "individuality" in Catholic countries as if the preservation of one's dignity sprang from some hidden mystical source.[68] Rather, I would suggest dignity is a form of capital that one cannot afford to squander. Like credit with the bank, it assures the flow of followers. Franklin asked the capitalist to "remember that *credit* is money." Per-haps a parallel for caudillaje man would be to "remember that dignity is followership." [69]

Dignity rests upon a wholly rational attitude toward life. Com-pacted to its essence, dignity requires a form of asceticism. It is self-denying in that one must rigidly control his outward behavior to achieve the desired effect. Passing tourists have made much of the spontaneity of caudillaje cultures. Yet fidelity to the culture as it exists finds the public man involved in a continuous attempt to foresee events and control his own external actions. Manuel Sánchez has understood this well: "Growing up in our environment here, we see the realities of life so close that we must learn to have a lot of self-control.... I have learned to hide my fear and to show only courage because from what I have observed, a person is treated according to the impression he makes." [70] One's dignity must be ever preserved because "dignity" constitutes a shorthand way of saying man's public or external face. The capitalistic tourists, for example, may perceive only public men dancing and clapping hands. Yet they are observing a profound competition between persons for public acknowledgment of their individual merits. "If the girl was a good dancer, those in the circle would send in another boy to show off what he could do. There really was atmosphere. Everybody tried to make himself stand out among the rest." [71] Such ability can contribute to one's success in acquiring and keeping a *clientela*. Ignazio Silone provides an excellent portrayal of individual merit in his novel, *Fontamara*. Don Circostanza has been given the title, "The People's Friend." But, as an old man, the narrator of the story, said, "Don Circonstanza had already cheated us hundreds of times, of course. But he had always had such a warmhearted, friendly way of going about it; he shook hands with everyone and when he was drunk he would even embrace them. We had always forgiven him, the more so because we needed his protection." [72] In these few words one sees the essence of caudillaje power relationships: the needs of followers and the power of the leader cemented together by the dignity of the latter.

A word that to some extent summarizes and encompasses all the public virtues is *manliness*—"the way in which a person asserts his own personality, the energy and tenacity with which he strives to affirm himself in front of others." [73] In caudillaje culture this term does partially synthesize and reduce the meaning inherent in other words such as dignity, grandeur, and generosity, since manliness has a broader signification than any of these. It is comparable for caudillaje man to the capitalist's virtues of thriftness and hard work. Manliness provides a structure within which caudillaje men may compete. Its importance stems from the fact that it furnishes an acceptable criterion for leader-follower relations. "He in whom authority is vested must possess the necessary manliness in order that he may be submitted to without humiliation," states one observer of Spain.[74] Participants in the manliness test, both dominated and the dominator, can feel comfortable in their respective roles.

One of the more specific meanings of manliness is physical prowess. Because the ethic is public, physical qualities reflecting an exclusively public orientation are naturally valued and practiced. Caudillaje man excels in those physical virtues that involve essentially solo performances and may be observed by the many. Such an orientation can be seen in the public man's choice of sports. Team efforts do not interest him so much as individual virtuosity—thus the importance of soccer throughout caudillaje culture. The game of soccer presupposes two competing teams while allowing for maximum exposure of individual competence on the playing field. In other words, it meets the prerequisite of the public man in a public forum. And, parenthetically, it is interesting to note that Brazil's *futebol* position began to decline after 1962 because "in Europe, led by England, a new concept of 'scientific' *futebol* began to dominate, based on defense, conditioning, and team discipline rather than improvisation and individual brilliance." [75]

In less formal settings, sporting events provide opportunities for bantering and camaraderie that may consolidate aggregations. That behavior contrasts distinctly with the competitive grimness often characterizing sports in Protestant-ethos countries, for example, Little League baseball. Hughes, in his *French Canada in Transition*, contrasts the French Canadian (Catholic) and English (Protestant) styles of play —the former being vibrant, the latter serious. In Cantonville, he says, there exists "a wide and deep gulf between French and English manners. . . . English tennis players play deep and drive hard; the chopping, tricky, bantering play of the French annoys them to distraction and often beats them. Similar complaints are made about golf. For the French, games and sports are always the occasion for lively social interplay. For the English, they are serious business." [76]

Or consider bullfighting, national sport of many caudillaje nations. No game could better depict the nature of the public man, his goals, and the means to those goals. Here more than in any other sport one publicly puts his life at stake to win applause from his fellowman. Either his excellence will see him triumph, or his ineptness will lead to failure. But in either case "the shedding of blood that goes on is a dramatic reminder that the bullfighters are taking a chance on losing their lives and the demonstrations of the huge crowd are an equally spectacular reminder of what the bullfighters stand to gain." [77] Unlike sports in capitalist countries, bullfighting does not revolve exclusively around finances, but around the central fact of life itself.[78] The bullfighter and those living his life vicariously as observers are engaged in the struggle of public virtue, in this case physical and mental prowess, pitted against the strongest symbol of nature, the bull. The torero's dexterity, agility, and judgment will shape public opinion within the arena and determine in large part his fame and name. In this sense, bullfighting symbolizes today the great achievements of public men throughout the history of caudillaje society.[79]

In ideal-typical form these manly feats often have military overtones such as those formerly exhibited at the head of armies. José Martí, the Cuban hero, described a famous Venzuelan caudillo, José Antoñio Páez: "When he was only a sergeant in his own ranks, the enemy, victorious in 1813, wanted him as a captain of cavalry. Was it not he who unseated thirty riders in one encounter? Was he not the 'pal,' the 'old man,' the 'boss' of the plainsmen whom he dazzled with his bravery, strength and shrewdness? Was it not he who could see a league's distance, kill the wild boar with a single arrow, master the wild pony with a fixed look, and send the bull sprawling with a twist of the tail?" [80] Or take the example of Juan Manuel Rosas who captured the peasants' imagination through physical and mental dexterity: "He surpassed them all in feats of activity and address, in taming wild horses, and in throwing the lasso." [81] Contemporary Brazilian novelist João Guimarães Rosa portrays a backlands hero:

The men did not deny him the fullest respect. Because he was all man. Ah, Ze Bebelo was plenty tough—seven daggers with seven blades, all in one sheath! He could handle any firearm and his aim was deadly; he could rope steers and ride the range as well as any cowboy; he could break the wildest animal—mule or horse; he could fight a knife duel with the cunning of a cornered wildcat, on the aggressive every moment; fear, and all the little relatives of fear, he spat upon and despised. They say he would wade in, and quell any fracas. Rough and tough, a man with guts! And to him, nothing seemed really impossible. [82]

Here is one face of the ethos of caudillaje in a world in which "the only thing of value is manliness, personal strength, a capacity for imposing oneself on others." [83] Transferred from the nineteenth-century plains of South America, one hears Che Guevara lauding the merits of a contemporary caudillo:

Fidel is a man of such great personal qualities that in whatever movement he participates he takes command. . . . He has the qualities of a great leader, which when added to his audacity, strength, courage, and untiring perseverance in discovering the will of the people, have taken him to the place of honor and personal sacrifice which he occupies today. He has other important qualities, such as a capacity to assimilate knowledge and experience quickly, to

understand the totality of a given situation without losing sight
of details, an unbounded faith in the future, and a breadth of vision
which allows him to see further and more accurately into the future than his comrades.[84]

Manliness as the drive for power characterizes all classes—it constitutes a cultural ethos in a holistic sense. Richard Adams writes with
insight into relationships among the Latin American upper class.

When Eric Wolf characterized the emergent *mestizo* population
of the past century and a half as "the power seekers," he correctly
identified power as the crucial feature of the upper sector. It is
left for us to add, however, that power-seeking is not limited to
the *mestizos* in the upper sector. The nature of power is something
that one can seldom depend upon having; power is a process that
exists as a part of many relationships, and anyone who fails to keep
that process going may suddenly find himself without it. Wolf's
characterization should, therefore, be extended to the entire upper
sector. It would not be an exaggeration to say that the entire internal structure of the upper sector is a series of relationships established and altered by virtue of a constant concern for gaining and
using power.[85]

I would extend his statements to constitute (1) an entire cultural ethos
covering all social classes and (2) an ethos that is free of the geographical bounds of Latin America. To Adams's and Wolf's limited focus
upon upper-class power one could, for example, call attention to Díaz's
description of the poor Mexican village of Tonalá. Here "in the Tonalá
social universe to be powerful is to be male. The effective political
leader is the independent *macho* who can command that things be done.
It is within his power to bestow favors, and it is also within his power
to withhold them. Since being a powerful leader requires at least the
tacit recognition of his role as a strong man, a leader who does not
assume some of the outward aspects of the *macho* role can get nothing
done." [86]

Both great political goals and great economic goals encourage certain deception and compromise of principle as part of the means necessary to achieve one's end. The Protestant ethos embraced such deception and rationalized it as behaviorally justified due to the greatness
of the goal of salvation. Thus wealth, the assurance of salvation, could

best be gained through presenting the proper "appearance" before one's creditors. By Franklin's time the virtues leading to wealth had taken on a distinctly utilitarian nature. "In order to secure my character and credit as a tradesman, I took care not only to be in *reality* industrious and frugal, but to avoid all appearances to the contrary. I drest plainly; I was seen at no places of idle diversion." [87] With regard to his attempt to gain a measure of humility, he said, "I cannot boast of much success in acquiring the *reality* of this virtue, but I had a good deal with regard to the appearance of it." [88] Max Weber beautifully summarized this ethos of appearances:

> Now all Franklin's moral attitudes are colored with utilitarianism. Honesty is useful, because it assures credit; so are punctuality, industry, frugality, and that is the reason they are virtues. A logical deduction from this would be that where, for instance, the appearance of honesty serves the same purpose, that would suffice, and an unnecessary surplus of this virtue would evidently appear to Franklin's eyes as unproductive waste. And as a matter of fact, the story in his autobiography of his conversion to those virtues, or the discussion of the value of a strict maintenance of the appearance of modesty, the assiduous belittlement of one's own deserts in order to gain general recognition later, confirms this impression. According to Franklin, those virtues, like all others, are only in so far virtues as they are actually useful to the individual, and the surrogate of mere appearance is always sufficient when it accomplishes the end in view.[89]

The necessity of emphasizing this deception or utilitarianism in the actions of Protestants is to show of how little consequence are the virtues of work, honesty, and frugality, per se, as compared to the end of making money. These outward attributes are absolutely essential, however, in that they enable one to more easily achieve the goal, namely, wealth. I think that Calvin, by posing the prize of salvation as the only acceptable end for every man, and yet, through the doctrine of predestination, closing the door to human acts as means toward this salvation, created a world style of "appearances." There is a sentence in his *Institutes* that is particularly revealing: "For the question is not how we can be righteous, but how, though unrighteous and unworthy, we can be considered as righteous." [90] Protestant man simply could not live with such uncertainty of election. He readily sought rational ways through which he could "be considered as righteous."

Capitalism is rooted in the Protestant version of prudence. Morality is connected to a floating mean. Adam Smith's *Theory of Moral Sentiments*, for example, has too often been ignored by those who seek to understand the basis of the Western work ethic. Smith in his essay on virtue discusses prudence: "The prudent man is always sincere, and feels horror at the very thought of exposing himself to the disgrace which attends upon the detection of falsehood. But though always sincere, he is not always frank and open, and, though he never tells anything but the truth, he does not always think himself bound, when not properly called upon to tell the whole truth." [91]

Caudillaje also utilizes appearances as a means for attaining one's goal of power and in demonstrating one's excellence. Perhaps it was inevitable that once public virtue became the criterion of superiority men should concentrate upon giving the "appearance" of possessing virtuous qualities. The always quotable Machiavelli stated it nicely: "It is not, therefore, necessary for a prince to have all the above-named qualities, but it is very necessary to seem to have them. I would even be bold to say that to possess them and always to observe them is dangerous, but to appear to possess them is useful." [92] Public virtue now becomes more understandable. It is the appearance of virtue that the public man must exhibit. A prudent display of excellence will decide the outcome; therefore, the major tool utilized by contending men will be their ability to gain favor for their claim to embody the appropriate virtues: "for the great majority of mankind are satisfied with appearances, as though they were realities, and are often even more influenced by the things that seem than those that are." [93] The public man can endeavor to surround himself with friends as a sure sign of virtue. Love for bureaucratic procedures, secretaries, stamps, seals, dark glasses, and long lines of people waiting to see *el jefe* all attest to caudillaje man's concrete need to give the appearance of these special qualities.

Caudillaje man developed indicators, one might say a "code of pretentions," of public power, just as Protestant-capitalistic man created signs of private wealth. These were in both cases designed to bear witness to or give "proof" of excellence. One does not surround himself with friends or gain economic advantage only from the actual practice of suitable virtues, but one must always give the appearance of possessing the appropriate excellence. For example, an Italian villager says, "the only way they'll respect you is the old *'Lei non sa chi sono io!'* You don't know who *I* am. Everything is privilege and bluff here. The more supercilious you are, the more important you must be." [94]

Or take, for example, the issue of wealth. Presumably a public man will have money. "But if a man or a nation does not have the virtues and opportunities necessary to conquer and amass wealth, what is he or it to do? The art of appearing rich has been cultivated in Italy as nowhere else." [95] The author of these lines then cites the aristocratic families without money who try to keep up pretenses by hiring coaches or giving parties once a year while nearly starving in between. Spaniards are famous for their "code of pretentions." Díaz-Plaja writes, "If in a sensible country the people first eat enough and *afterwards* dress themselves, the Spaniard first adorns himself with every elegance, even when his alimentation leaves much to be desired, because this latter no one sees." [96] Here one discerns in striking tones a habit of appearances common to all caudillaje society. The Quixote legend characterizes the ethos: appearance of title, wealth, and an elevated code of public honor. In that lies caudillaje man's "quest," as Richard Kiley sings in the Broadway version of *Man of La Mancha*. One hardly needs, however, to refer to aristocracy or legend to observe the practice of appearing. For example, what could be more public than the clothes one wears? Thus, caudillaje blue-collar labor, from factory workers to garbage collectors, will often travel to and from work wearing a necktie and carrying tools, lunch, or work clothes in a briefcase. As a tie designates status, that is, a sign of individual worth, so he wears one proudly to give the appearance of position. Or, recall the organization of the home —arranged in such a way as to convey the public impression of wealth or status even though these may be lacking.

The public man thus becomes of necessity the man of many masks. Within a power situation, he may seek to emulate a Rosas. It was the Argentine tyrant Juan Manuel Rosas who "displayed with rare perfection, anger, frankness, and bonhomie"; he was a person who "when encountered face to face . . . could intimidate, or deceive, or seduce." [97] Strongly bedded in the culture, this type of behavior has become formalized and hallowed.[98]

Thus, instead of a rigid practicing of the virtues of generosity, dignity, grandeur, leisure, and manliness, one often sees only the appearance of these virtues in caudillaje society. Grandeur is reduced to ostentation; dignity becomes posturing and rigid formalism. (After a ten-minute rest stop, passengers on an Italian bus were allowed to reenter—but most of them did so by the wrong door and were turned out again. "There was a door at the front and a door at the back; the one at the front, the conductor explained reverently, was for passengers entering, that at the rear for passengers dismounting. Although they were actually inside the bus when their mistake was discovered, they climbed down again and trooped around to the front.")[99] Generosity takes on a calculating give-and-receive quality; leisure gives way to public sunning. (I can recall a literal example from an isolated beach in Costa Rica. With no one on the beach except a North American and his girl friend, a bored Latin and his son began to play Frisbee. Play moves closer and closer to the North Americans. The father struts back and forth; soon he goes back to his cabin to return a short time later in new bathing trunks—all activity, every movement calculated to impress the only people on the beach—who wanted only to be left alone.)[100] And manliness, the summary virtue, degenerates into a variation on the theme of *machismo*.

Now manliness implicitly has connotations of virility. It is worth noting that in Latin "virtue" means virility.[101] Virtue seen as manliness has historically carried implications of masculinity. Cicero, that favorite author of caudillaje man, stated the theory in all its simplicity: "Whatever is done with a stout and virile spirit seems proper and worthy of a real man; whatever act is characterized by the opposite spirit is both evil and improper." [102] One person who projected this robust image into Spanish culture was El Cid, the medieval folk hero. "El Cid possesses all the qualities characteristic of those who have to impose themselves to triumph: strength of arm and heart, valor, prudence, cunning and ingenuity; in brief, physical and moral vigor." [103] Not surprisingly, in some present-day caudillaje societies the doctrine of public virtue or manliness has been subsumed under the term *machismo*. And while machismo primarily connotes virility, more generally speaking, it applies to persons who appear to personify in their conduct the virtues of grandeur, generosity, and dignity—indicators of public excellence.

Caudillaje finds in machismo the functional equivalent for the Protestant ethic's emphasis upon hard work.[104] "Regardless of social position," writes Gillin, "the *macho* is admired. The cultural concept involves sexual prowess, action orientation (including verbal action), and various other components." [105] A propensity toward machismo naturally runs counter to the traditional Catholic emphasis in religious pageantry upon the Christ crucified and broken. (Poor peasants may more easily relate to Christ because he can serve as one with whom they can identify—one who is equally beaten and set upon by those in authority. "Christ is El Macho turned inside out," as one author says.)[106] Rev. Leo T. Mahon outlines the problem:

I submit that we unwittingly tend to propose to men Christ as a person to be loved directly, absolutely and without qualification whatsoever. The true man is repelled by such a suggestion. Those less masculine may not be so repelled and there may be some who may even like it. Haven't we sometimes wondered why the most manly Catholic men in the neighborhood do not seem to be particularly fervent in their faith while the less manly men are very often very much in evidence at parish services and meetings? In recent times we have witnessed an horrendous effeminization of Christ in religious art and popular devotion.[107]

In all probability tension between macho values in the public sphere and the obvious effeminate nature of Christ in the world of religion accounts for the low public church attendance of Catholic men—and may be counterposed to continued strong support for Catholicism at home, in the education of their children and as preferred values for their wives. Private religion obviously cannot serve Catholics as a basis for public behavior. For example, Nelson, in *The Waiting Village*, considers members of the Holy Family as having symbolic representation within the rural community. She concludes, "whereas it is quite clear that the Virgin functions as the females' ego ideal par excellence, there is no equally clear counterpart for the male. Joseph, for all the respect accorded him, is looked upon as a cuckold; God is too distant to be clearly perceived as a role model; and Christ, for all his compassion—or because of it—is effeminate." [108] According to another writer, in Spain "Catholicism has undergone matriarchal changes to such a point that God the Father and God the Creator have been almost totally suppressed. On the one hand, God the Son is the incarnation of weakness, of the falling away and of death; on the other, the obsessive beating of drums underscores the majestic presence—on the altar or on the processional float slowly propelled by the throng—of the goddess-mother, sparkling with precious stones, the miraculous and omniscient idol polarizing all the mystic fervor of the race." [109] Finally, Díaz-Plaja capsulizes the public macho attitude when confronted with the private institutionalized value structure. "The Spaniards," he says, "are more capable of dying in defense of the door of a church than of entering it." [110]

One might say that homilies like those found in *Poor Richard's Almanac* built the United States; and one would be equally correct in observing that machismo and its variants built caudillaje society. As has been observed, "The Spaniard goes to the street every morning disposed to demonstrate to the world how masculine he is."[111] From the era of the conquistadores, who came to the New World to prove they were men, until today, it is machismo which seems to count for most in caudillaje culture.[112] And one should take cognizance of the fact that the macho tradition presumes the submission of people—the domination of man by man,[113] while the capitalist tradition takes for granted the subjugation of nature—domination of the environment by man.[114] Self-worth in the latter case typically depends upon one's ability to dominate the physical environment (for example, as North Americans were once characterized by their agrarian ways, they are now defined by their scientistic disposition—both rooted in mastery of the laws of an always challenging nature); while in the first instance individual worth stands contingent upon one's expertise in manipulating social relationships (for example, winning out in a social milieu that a writer on Poland says had been presented to him from birth as "a constant and rather cruel interplay of domination and subordination.")[115] Here, of course, as throughout this book, I am painting the picture with a very broad brush—ignoring the multitude of qualifications. But if one looks in on the activities of those first representatives of each culture to come to the New World, the difference is obvious: Pilgrims concerned themselves with planting, harvesting, and clearing the land, that is, the domination of nature; conquistadores (the word means "conquerors") set about the political-social and economic organization of the native population, that is, the domination of peoples. True, exploitation of man by man did occur, as Marx so readily reminds us, when Protestant-capitalist man with his private, exploitative, capital-accruing ethic sought to dominate these impersonal forces of nature. But personal domination was only a means to the goal of capital accumulation, not an end in itself. As such, with automation personalized exploitation could possibly decline in Protestant ethic societies. Catholic man, by contrast, has consciously sought to subdue people, because public virtue comes measured in terms of the scope of one's control over persons. As a result, while Protestant man alternately ignored the Indian and then stole his land, Catholic man not only put the Indians to serving his table but also organized them into personal armies—seeking to bind them to him by becoming God-father to his children.

Thus, an inclination to dispose of other people's lives has remained a salient part of the Catholic ethos. Ideally, like the conquistador, caudillaje man will neither do, nor know how to do, any physical work, just as the *patrón* traditionally did not labor. "Does a *misti* [*patrón*] know how to irrigate a field or to fence a meadow? Does he know how to weed wheatfields or repair a road? Can he make tiles or adobe bricks, or even so much as kill a sheep?" [116] a Peruvian novelist asks rhetorically. Ciro Alegría in his classic book, *El mundo es ancho y ajeno*, answers through Don Alvaro: no, the *patrón* should only direct others' efforts. "It's a sacred debt I owe my father's memory. Besides, Peru needs men of enterprise who will make people work. What's the good of all this cheap humanitarianism? It's work and more work, and so that there will be work there must be men who will make the masses work." [117]

Everyman can give the appearance of being the man of public virtue by being macho. Again, I would stress the classless nature of the ethos. Machismo cuts across society and is evident everywhere. "The Latin American male fancies himself as a sort of rooster; he is proud of his prowess in many respects. The upper- and middle-class male will maintain the *casa chica*, the little house where his mistress lives. In the lower classes, *machismo* manifests itself in plural free unions." [118] And I would reiterate my belief that stages of economic growth are largely irrelevant to this phenomenon. That machismo cannot be linked to a temporary state of economic development has been tellingly underscored by one observer's discussion of driving habits in Latin America.

The psychologists concerned with traffic accidents have come to the conclusion (plausible in the light of common sense) that the manner of driving depends on and reveals the entire personality of the driver. If one applies this principle to the Latin Americans, one must conclude that their chief characteristic is brutal and blind pursuit of momentary advantage; they drive with utter disregard for the safety of others and with very little concern for their own or for the safety of their vehicles. . . . Courtesy on the road is entirely unknown: nobody ever stops or slows down to let somebody else turn or get in or out, and the biggest vehicle, which can do most damage, always has the right-of-way regardless of the rules of the road. The selfishness of the opulent classes shows itself in utter disregard for the safety and comfort of the pedestrians on the country roads. As there are no lanes for pedestrians, despite the fact that they are much more numerous than the travelers in motor vehicles, they must wade through stones and sand, and on occasion jump into ditches to avoid being killed. These habits cannot be simply due to the embryonic stage of industrialization because the country which is most developed economically—Argentina—has the worst reputation for brutal driving. A comparison of Argentina with Britain or Holland thirty years ago shows that reckless driving cannot be a mere consequence of novelty or the smaller number of cars.[119]

Caudillaje man is as assiduous in cultivating his macho image as Protestant man is diligent in maintaining his work image.[120] Thus, the common man demonstrates his public virtue by possessing many children, by having or pretending to have a mistress. In addition, he wants to protect his *dignidad* on every occasion. Above all, he strives to maintain a great formalism behind which any private weaknesses can be hidden and which will lend ponderous weight to his position, pronouncements, and authority.

The most singular feature of the virtue of manliness lies in its connotations of power. The macho is "power isolated in its own potency," as Octavio Paz phrased it.[121] Although one could easily overstate here, the power orientation of caudillaje society almost always has a sexual referent.[122] As Salvadore Allende Gossens, the late Marxist president of Chile, in giving his opinion of former President Eduardo Frei, said, "the difference between Frei and me is that I have balls and he doesn't." [123] In focusing upon the dominance aspect of caudillaje culture, we are marking out a central concern of public men: "that longing for power that we all carry within ourselves." [124] The drive to fulfill that longing structures life in those lands from cradle to grave.[125] For example, in the matter of mistresses alluded to earlier one sees the power orientation of caudillaje culture. Contrary to the non-caudillaje movie version of romance, the macho has absolutely no interest in giving love or affection to a woman other than his wife. Love implies a certain softness, sensibility, concern for one's partner's welfare—preoccupations wholly contrary to the conception of power and virility. "To be *macho* coincides more with sex than with love. The trajectory is simple. If one *possesses* a woman, he is a man. But if one *loves* a woman, he is weak and even a 'fool.' " [126] In fact, the private sexual act itself becomes of secondary importance in caudillaje society; it is the public demonstration of "owning" a beautiful woman that takes first priority. Hence, the interminable parade of one's mistress about town signifies a man's virility, success—namely, manliness. To promenade one's beautiful wife—something almost unheard of in these lands—

could only indicate the debilitating constraints of love (although it is useful to one's image for people to know that a beautiful, wellborn, and utterly ornamental wife awaits at home).

Another example of a culture tied to man's longing for power is furnished by the commercial press. Newspapers in caudillaje society run constant advertisements extolling various products designed to aid the common man in his quest for virility. Following is an example taken from *La prensa*, Managua, Nicaragua.

Good news for MEN: *opovitam* (with testicular extract) reinforces virile vigor. *Opovitam*, manufactured according to a new and better formula . . . is a new product composed of testicular extract and other masculine sexual glandular substances, that establish and reinforce the virile capacity in men prematurely fading [*decaidos*].

Opovitam is very effective in cases of sexual weakness, states of physical and emotional depression, lack of memory, fatigue or mental weariness, and other symptoms characteristic of premature declining in MAN.

Return to feeling young and spirited toward everyone.

Reinforce your Virile Vigor; ask in Pharmacies and Begin today to take OPOVITAM, *for men*.[127]

One who practices manliness (public virtue) presumably would accomplish great public deeds. The surest sign of merit would entail the holding of formalized public power. Those Romans extolled in caudillaje society's history books are almost without exception power holders. In seeking public position as a sign of his worth, caudillaje man quite naturally attempts to emulate that history. Consider then Virgil's Roman classic, the *Aeneid*: "the heroes there are not human beings, but bigger, stronger, grander." [128] The kind of eulogizing common in works by Roman historians may be seen in Livy's portrayal of the character of Marcus Porcius Cato:

There was no art, in either personal or civic affairs of which he was not a master. He handled with equal skill the business of the city and of the country. Some men have been advanced to high position by knowledge of the law, others by the power of eloquence, others by military genius. But his ability was so perfectly adapted to all kinds of achievement that whatever he put his hand to seemed to be his special fight. In war he was a mighty soldier, distinguished in many battles; but when advanced to a position of command he was unmatched as a general. In peace he was a most learned interpreter of the law, if there was need for legal advice, or if a case was to be defended, a most eloquent advocate.[129]

In an earlier work, Livy described the character of Hannibal noting that he was the most worthy man to put in charge of any assignment "which demanded bravery and vigor." Hannibal was the "best among cavalry and infantry alike, always the first to go into battle and the last to leave any clash of arms." [130] Suetonius, through his portraits of the twelve Caesars plays upon this same theme. Caesar, we are told, "was highly skilled in arms and horsemanship, and of incredible powers of endurance. On the march he headed his army, sometimes on horseback, but oftener on foot, bareheaded both in the heat of sun and in rain. He covered great distances with incredible speed, making a hundred miles a day in a hired carriage and with little baggage, swimming the rivers which barred his path or crossing them on inflated skins, and very often arriving before the messengers sent to announce his coming." [131]

Roman ideals such as the foregoing pervade caudillaje countries and reinforce the system of public virtue. By way of indicating the influence which these notions had upon the Renaissance genesis of this ethos, I cite Machiavelli writing of Castruccio Castracani: "First of all, he [Castruccio] made himself an excellent rider, managing even the most fiery horse with the greatest skill; and in jousts and tournaments, though he was a mere boy, he was more notable than anybody else, so that in every feat, whether of strength or skill, no man could be found who surpassed him." [132] Another Renaissance writer, Matteo Palmieri, approvingly repeats this view of antiquity. "Greek, Roman, and Barbarian history," he says, "is full of memorable examples which show how the noble citizens manfully disdained every personal comfort for the well-being of the republic—for which deeds they were made famous with highest glory and immortalized in the world with everlasting fame." [133] Through its continued celebration of great public men of the past, caudillaje thus inextricably reinforces in men's minds the equation of manly virtue with public power holders. This equation is not readily forgotten: the most virtuous man is still perceived as the one who can take and hold public power.

The necessity of keeping power once it has been attained is of great importance for understanding the nature of politics in caudillaje nations. Carlos Fuentes elucidates: "The Revolution can satisfy them now, but tomorrow they may ask for more and more and what would we have left to offer if we should give everything already? Except, perhaps, our lives: and why die if we thereby do not live to see the beneficent fruits of our heroic deaths? We are men, not martyrs: if we hold on to power, nothing will not be permitted: lose power and they'll fuck us: have a sense of destiny, we are young and we glitter with successful armed revolution: why have we fought, to die of hunger? When force is necessary, it is justified: power may not be divided." [134] Respect and submission to power holders even pervades the fantasy life of caudillaje peoples.[135] A Mexican villager, asked to make up a story to fit a picture of "older man and profile of young man," says the older man "tries to convince the boy that he has to dominate, to instill fear, to show the students that he's the boss, that he is strong. He has to win out. If he lets them win, he is lost." [136] Another maintains that the villagers "will follow anyone who will lead them; they are like sheep. What these people follow is power. He who holds power over these people is the one they believe. The priest has great power because he uses fear to control the people—he threatens excommunication." [137]

To be a private doctor, lawyer, or general is not a sufficient indication of worth—only public power can fully gratify his desire, as the economic category "millionaire" can perhaps only approach gratification of Protestant ethic man's sense of total achievement. In the end both spell self-worth and are their own justification. As Don Artemio put the matter: "Power is worthwhile in itself, this I know." [138]

But for most people in caudillaje society the near impossibility of holding a tangible high office is surely paralleled by an equally remote opportunity for the masses of capitalistic culture in their quest to become millionaires. Not all men can take political power, nor can all men become wealthy. According to the tenets of the Protestant ethic only a small part of mankind is destined for salvation. Yet as salvation was an otherworldly phenomenon and one's election was always in doubt, hard work leading to material gain opened at least the appearance of salvation to everyman. No doubt in this fashion began the anxiety-ridden status seeking so common to middle-class America. With his eye ever upon his neighbor's house, garage, and general wealth, Protestant man began the secularized equivalent of salvation: economic gain.

Caudillaje man, similarly, could on a personal ego basis endeavor to win deference and respect by showing himself to be the man of public power, just as his Protestant counterpart could realize himself by striving to publicly appear to be saved. The means in the one case came to be hard work, in the other manliness, machismo. Manliness is egalitarian in its promise, just as the rags-to-riches Horatio Alger philosophy can sustain capitalistic man in hope and aspiration. It is this thought which Machiavelli conveys when encouraging his fellowmen: "Let no one, then, fear not to be able to accomplish what others have done, for all men . . . are born and live and die in the same way, and therefore resemble each other." [139] A more contemporary statement comes from Salvador de Madariaga who has noted the culturewide tendency toward personalism in Spain which "leads to dictatorship, observable not merely in the public man, statesman, general, cardinal, or king at the head of the state, but in every one of the men at the head (or on the way thereto) of every village, city, region, business firm, or even family in the country." [140] Here lies the tendency born of an ethos where the son takes pride in his father because "he is a man who knows how to command respect; he's well known and he can make men obey him and fear him." [141]

Generalizing upon a Protestant anxiety that flows from an uncertain salvation, I have concluded that John Gillin errs in his contention that "a 'real *macho*' is one who is sure of himself, cognizant of his own inner worth, and willing to bet everything on such self-confidence. . . . The *macho* may express his own inner conviction by overt action, as in the case of bandits and 'revolutionary' military leaders, or he may do so verbally, as in the case of a leading intellectual, lawyer, or politician." [142] On the contrary, I believe the public man takes overt action precisely because of a *lack* of confidence in his own inner worth. Through public action he endeavors (as does his Protestant counterpart) to demonstrate to himself that he has this worth. Santiago Ramírez, in *El mexicano, psicología de sus motivaciones*, comes much closer to the truth when he says "at base the *machismo* of the Mexican is nothing but an insecurity over one's own masculinity; the ornamentation [*el barroquismo*] of virility." For, says Ramírez, "the man spends his income or the major part of it in emphasizing his masculine status, and he is terribly fond of all those articles of clothing symbolic of masculinity: the hat, be it cowboy or Italian [*borsalino*]; the pistol, horse or automobile will be his magnificence and pride; intended for those external manifestations to which he compulsively reverts in order to affirm a strength that he inwardly lacks." [143]

Caudillaje men can, as compared to capitalists, find themselves in an even more difficult position, "anxious as they are to demonstrate prowess and manliness." [144] Public virtue is a this-worldly concept. A man of true virtue or manliness would presumably emerge as a leader of other men: in the formal sense of power this could mean at least becoming a humble village *alcalde*.[145] But these positions are even more limited in quantity than Protestant estimates as to the number of the "elect" within their midst. Worse, the results are publicly known: a man of virtue who becomes president of his nation has more certainly attained his goal than a man of wealth who *may* also be saved. Fulfillment or failure is evident in the one case but only speculative in the other. It may be for this reason that Catholic men have often come to actually shun politics and public life,[146] just as capitalistic man in the twentieth century frequently seeks to avoid the competition of the marketplace. It would be a mistake, however, to assume in either case that the traditional virtues are dead.

In short, I am maintaining that to practice the virtue of machismo, personalism, manliness—whatever word one would choose—constitutes wholly rational activity for the public man.[147] Yet it is perhaps relevant to note the behavior of men when public virtue fails to accomplish the power goals toward which they strive. Durkheim's study of suicide sheds light upon the consequences of such failure—and in the process adds another dimension to the caudillaje-capitalistic dichotomy.

It was Durkheim who pointed out that "Catholicism reduces the tendency to suicide while Protestantism increases it," while also noting that "inversely, homicides are much more frequent in Catholic countries than among Protestant peoples." [148] The capitalist with his inner-directed private virtues resolves a very large crisis in the same manner in which he has lived. That is, he turns toward himself to consummate his final "deal," the last act of a self-made man. The Richard Cory poem of Edwin Arlington Robinson says it well. Caudillaje man, in contrast, lives by public virtues and, if he must, will prefer to die by those virtues. Failure to succeed will more readily lead him to homicide—to "conquer" his opponent whatever may be the consequences.[149] In this sense homicide is indeed a form of public suicide, for one kills and damns the cost. Nor will individual regrets or private recriminations be likely to cloud his act of murder. Only public shame could lead to second thoughts about one's behavior.[150] One's last free act thus becomes an exercise in power over others. But should caudillaje man choose suicide, more than likely it will entail a public display. Unlike the capitalist who, in his parsimonious fashion commits suicide as he lives—by a last act of will over his own body—and usually in a rather private fashion, caudillaje man is more likely to go down in a blaze of glory. Getulio Vargas, for example, killed himself while still president of Brazil. In his suicide note he compares himself to another Savior: "My sacrifice shall remain forever in your soul and my blood be the price of your redeeming." [151]

Observations upon the nature of caudillaje society could be expanded. But in order to more fully understand this phenomenon I turn to an examination of causality. What, one may ask, could contribute to the existence of a spirit of caudillaje in the geographical areas of Latin America, Spain, Poland, Portugal, Ireland, France, French Canada, Hungary, Austria, Romania and Italy? The most obvious factor uniting these lands is their similitude of religious outlook and tradition. Culturally they are almost monolithically Catholic. Each remained essentially untouched by the Reformation and each was subjected to the Counter Reformation. Despite inroads of Protestantism in more recent times, they continue as Catholic societies. And it is here that we will look for a plausible explanation for the spirit of caudillaje. In the following chapter an attempt will be made to demonstrate the causal link between Catholicism and caudillaje.

III

RELIGIOUS FOUNDATIONS
OF PUBLIC VIRTUE

In looking at public life within the Catholic world, one immediately notes the absence of what, in most of the West, one might call virtue. Tolerance, honesty, humility, willingness to compromise, frugality with public funds, service to the people seem to be missing—even as an ideal. Yet within the home or between friends one finds qualities of Christian virtue in abundance. The following observations on Italy could, I think, be extended to all of caudillaje society.

> One fundamental point which escapes most foreigners must be understood and remembered. Most Italians still obey a double standard. There is one code valid within the family circle with relatives and honorary relatives, intimate friends and close associates, and there is another code regulating life outside. Within, they assiduously demonstrate all the qualities which are not usually attributed to them by superficial observers: they are relatively reliable, honest, truthful, just, obedient, generous, disciplined, brave and capable of self-sacrifices. They practice what virtues other men usually dedicate to the welfare of their country at large; the Italians' family loyalty is their true patriotism. In the outside world, amidst the chaos and the disorder of society, they often feel compelled to employ the wiles of underground fighters in enemy-occupied territory. All official and legal authority is considered hostile by them until proved friendly or harmless: if it cannot be ignored, it should be neutralized or deceived if need be.[1]

One can better appreciate this double standard by pausing over Barzini's comments upon members of the Mafia. What he terms "visible lives" of the members of this prototypal caudillaje organization I would call their private lives: "In effect, the visible lives of the old high-ranking Mafia men are generally spotless. They are good fathers, good husbands, good sons; their word is sacred; they fastidiously refrain from having anything to do with spying, prostitution, drugs, or dishonest swindles. They never betray a friend. They are always devoted churchmen, who give large sums to the local parish or to the deserving poor. Many have sisters in convents and brothers in holy orders." [2] One could use much the same words to describe the guerrillas of the Latin America Left or Right of the past decade.

The separation between public and private extends to caudillaje architecture. "A house makes it possible to eat one's bread in privacy— and bread eaten in privacy is sweet, it teaches one wisdom—a house enjoys the safety of permanence and of being socially approved.... The street, on the other hand, is an unstable, dangerous, adventurous world, false as a looking-glass—the public laundry of all the dirty linen in the neighborhood." [3] The typical home faces inward with its courtyard in the center, protected from public view. I will anticipate the thesis spelled out in this chapter to note the difference here from the Protestant tradition where public and private are intermingled in their architectural styles. Protestant-ethic man can have his picture windows. Life in the Single City demands that no secrets be kept. In parts of western United States where the Protestant ethic perhaps more closely reflects its antecedents, shades are even left up at night. René de Visme Williamson states my theme in another way: "The family is the only human institution in which human relations are fully personal, and a house is the physical structure whose protective walls cut off impersonal and therefore alien intrusions. The Spanish word for getting married, *casarse*, is highly significant: it means 'to put oneself into a house,' hence a married woman is *casada* (housed in)." [4]

The importance of this bilevel theory of virtue cannot be overestimated. Here we have a primary reality of Catholic life—the separation of the ethical world into the public and the private. One is the ethic of the public, of politics, the other a private and religious ethic. And for the average family within caudillaje culture, the ideal father represents the values of the public sphere, while the ideal mother represents the values of the private religious sphere.[5] The Virgin Mary, symbol of both religiosity and motherhood, presides over the hearth, while the public sphere remains the province of the god of power.[6] It is for this reason that the popes of Rome have so little success when speaking upon public matters. When, for example, the Vatican attempted to intervene in Ireland's politics in the late nineteenth century by urging the Irish to rid themselves of their great Protestant leader, Charles Stuart Parnell, the Irish bishops refused to support the pope. Instead, they issued a statement to the effect that "while of course the Roman Pontiff had the right to speak with authority on faith and morals they were sure he did not intend to interfere with politics nor to injure the national movement." [7] Such events could be recounted endlessly throughout the caudillaje world.

Compare Protestant-ethic countries. In these societies one does not see such a clear or sharp differentiation of man's actions within the public and the private. Certainly Protestant man's acts in private are not always consistent with the public image which he would project. Yet one will look in vain for a double standard of morality itself. Stealing within the family is seen as evil; so also stealing from the public constitutes a wrong. Compromise, frugality, tolerance constitute virtues equally appropriate to the private and the public spheres of life. It must be remembered that in most cases these portray aspirations rather than reality. However, if one would seek to locate an emphasis in Protestant society, it would be found within the private. Henry David Thoreau typified capitalist values of the hearth when he said, "Now that the republic—the *res-publica*—has been settled, it is time to look after the *res-privata*—the private state." [8] His continued popularity attests to the importance of the private realm among North Americans. They agree, private self-interest should orient the life of God-fearing men.

Life, it is assumed by Catholic man, divides itself into two spheres, each with its own disparate moral code. Simón Bolívar, an archetypal caudillaje man, expounded this division: "The world is one thing, religion another. . . . The noble warrior, daring and fearless, stands out in sharpest contrast to the shepherd of souls." [9] Or, as another revolutionary, Fidel Castro, allowed: "Priests who do not carry out counter-revolutionary campaigns can teach religion, because religion is one thing and politics another." [10] Here we have a restatement of the hoariest of Catholic doctrines, the concept of the Two Cities.[11] According to this theory, public life is lived upon one set of ethical premises while private and religious life is based upon another. As the founder of modern Catholicism, Saint Thomas Aquinas (1225–74) put the matter, "the spiritual realm must be distinct from the earthly." [12] It allows those from caudillaje culture to feel no shame when hearing the Venetian ambassador, Simon Contarini, remark of the Spaniards, "they are essentially Catholic in religion but by no means moral in their conduct." [13] Religiosity and morality are never equated as in Protestant culture. Reviewing an article on religion by a North American, Robert Millikan, Julio Navarro Monzo of Argentina wrote: "Millikan lamentably confounds religion and morals, which are two distinct activities. Morality is an endeavor to accommodate the individual to collective life; religion is an endeavor to accommodate man to an order superior to himself." [14]

The world is divided into two realms, each with its own ethic. And consequent upon this ethical division arises a mode of life and public activity that invariably calls forth a personalistic style of leadership—men who act upon an ethical plain far removed from that laid down by the founders of the Christian religion. Such "non-Christian" activity of Machiavellian princes, of contemporary caudillos, of "everyman," is quite supportable under the concept of the Two Cities. Understanding of Catholic man's behavior rests upon an appreciation of this dualistic-ethic world view.

Conceptualization of the Two Cities originates with Saint Augustine's classical division between the values of the political world and those of religion. Augustine (354–430 A.D.) gives shape and substance to the idealistic admonitions of Saint Paul and Jesus. Christianity is an otherworldly religion. Apostolic spokesmen for primitive Christianity consistently affirmed this position. Saint Paul, for example, maintained that Christians were "citizens of heaven" (Phil. 3: 20) and "fellow-citizens of the saints" (Eph. 2: 19). A natural playing down of the importance of the things of this world and this life follows as a consequence of such a world view. In short, Christians are only "strangers and pilgrims" (1 Pet. 2: 11) on earth. Their true hope and allegiance stretch to another domain.

The Christian apocalypse signifies the futility of political action. Rewards are not to be found in public activity. Man is advised not to lay up treasure or seek power and glory on earth. It is the hypocrites who act that they may have glory of men (Matt. 6: 12). In fact, the clearest test of the primitive Christian's religiosity was to be found in his goal. Non-Christians and sinners were distinguished as those whose minds were "set on earthly things" (Phil. 2: 20). A Christian, by contrast, was one who recognized that his "reward is in Heaven" (Matt. 5: 12). Primitive Christianity, in effect, divided humanity into two

groups: political man and sinners on the one side with Christians on
the other.

While living in this world, Christians were directed to make their
peace with civil authorities. They were enjoined to remember that, as
there is no power but of God, the powers that be "are ordained by
God" (Rom. 13: 1). Therefore, every individual was encouraged to be
subject unto the higher powers. The New Testament of the primitive
Christians advised a policy of obedience, if not subservience, to civil
authority as a religious obligation.

From this dual stress upon worldly abnegation on the one hand
and otherworldly asceticism on the other, it follows that man has two
debts. He is called to "render unto Caesar the things which are Caesar's,
and unto God the things that are God's." In these few words, Jesus
charged his followers to make a sharp distinction between two types
of obligation. One debt is of the present world, that which is public
and belongs to Caesar. The other debt is aligned with the next world,
that which is private and belongs to God.

Thus was born what has been characterized as the "slave morality"
of early Christianity. Man was encouraged by his ethos to be poor,
meek, merciful, and a peacemaker if he would dwell with the blessed.
The focus is upon God's grace and man's future otherworldly life.

New Testament Christianity, in short, does not provide a positive
public ethic. Those who act as "publicans" are assured that they will
not enter the kingdom of God. It is those who act in *private* who shall
live in eternal blessedness. Because it is eschatological and apocalyptic
in character, New Testament Christianity says almost nothing about
political activism. Man awaiting his end, "dreading and hoping all" as
Yeats has put it, is encouraged to obey Caesar while acting out a
Christian life which looks for its justification to a heavenly reward.

The nonpolitical ethos of the Christian religion was abruptly
changed upon the conversion to Christianity of the emperor Constantine in the fourth century. Passage of the Edict of Milan (313 A.D.)
and introduction of the Nicene Creed guaranteed to Christians not only
participation within the political realm of the Roman Empire but the
preeminent role. Yet the dilemma of the primitive Church was not resolved. While Christians might act in a public setting, there was no
accepted rationale for such action. For the first thorough definition of
the dual role of Christian man, one must await the collapse of the
empire and the Church which had allied itself to the power structure
of that empire. When the barbarians were at the gates and Christians

were being charged with the undermining of Eternal Rome, a new synthesis and rationale were at last provided. Saint Augustine became the catalytic agent.

Augustine accomplishes his new vision by designating two realms, the *civitas terrena*, or Earthly City, and the *civitas Dei*, or City of God.[15] In formulating the issue in this manner, he follows an early Christian belief that man can be defined by his goal:

> Two cities have been formed by two loves; the earthly by the love of self, even to the contempt of God; the heavenly by the love of God even to the contempt of self. The former, in a word, glories in itself, the latter in the Lord. For the one seeks glory from men; but the greatest glory of the other is God, the witness or conscience. The one lifts up its head in its own glory; the other says to its God, "Thou art my glory and the lifter up of mine head." ... The one delights in its own strength, represented in the persons of its rulers; the other says of its God, "I will love Thee, O Lord, my strength." [16]

Those who strive after glory in the classical sense, he relegates to the Earthly City. But those who adhere to the New Testament gospel of love become candidates for the City of God.

Despite Augustine's belief in predestination and equation of the Two Cities with the community of the "saved" and the community of the "damned," and despite his recognition that "there are many reprobate mingled with the good," [17] the total effect of his theory is to link Christians with the organized Church and non-Christians with the political activities of the world. True, the life of the saints is social,[18] but they are only temporary sojourners in the world. Political action remains largely in the hands of the condemned. Augustine demonstrates this point by noting that Cain belonged to the City of Man, while Abel belonged to the City of God. And "it is recorded of Cain that he built a city, but Abel, being a sojourner, built none. For the city of the saints is above." [19] "Sojourners," "pilgrims," "wanderers," as he variously calls the citizens of the *civitas Dei*, have little time for political architectonics.

Public activity is not, however, prohibited to Christians by Augustine's synthesis. Those of the elect may be blending with the damned, trying to "pass." "We see now a citizen of Jerusalem, a citizen of the Kingdom of Heaven, holding some office upon earth; as for example, wearing the purple, serving as magistrate, as aedile, as proconsul, as Emperor, directing the earthly republic." Yet Augustine hastens to add, "but he hath his heart above if he is a Christian, if he is of the faithful, if he despiseth those things wherein he is and trusteth in that wherein he is not yet." [20] Thus early in the Catholic tradition was stated the sine qua non of a caudillaje world view: the division of the universe into Two Cities, each with its own ethic. And it is this division which underlies the lives of these areas today. Caudillaje man asserts unequivocally that the rules governing one's behavior in this world may be distinguished from the rules governing the behavior of the saints.

The significance of such dualism is this: caudillaje man does not endeavor to Christianize life outside the home as does his Protestant capitalistic counterpart. On the contrary, he accepts the fact that public pursuits have a set of rules and goals which are usually at odds with Christianity. And one who would participate in such activity, maintains the Catholic, must be willing to adopt the method, style, and ends of the City of Man. The public expediency, corruption, and apparent baseness of caudillaje life, for example, as well as the public actor's constant pursuit of worldly honor and use of lofty discourse suggest our conclusion. Caudillaje politics is very much the politics of *man*. And whether the Church is officially or unofficially united with the State, in practice the two are separated by a value chasm. The underlying philosophy of Catholicism supports this separation. [21]

By contrast, the Protestant ethic demands a single value structure for the public and religious spheres. Max Weber has demonstrated the manner in which Protestantism took over the values of the monastery and generalized them within the world. It was Martin Luther, the Augustinian monk, who in the first of his Ninety-five Theses maintained that Jesus had "called for the *entire life* of believers to be one of penitence." And it was this holistic endeavor that guided reforming Protestants who sought to found a pure Church made up of "visible saints." [22] While Protestants early attempted to become visible saints, Catholics sought to associate with the saints as a means of salvation. Hence, for example, Protestant churches were generally bare of statues, tapestries, carvings, and such—for of what need have "visible saints" of visible images of saints? Catholics, by contrast, living the less pretentious existence of the City of Man, have ever felt a need for empathy with various intermediaries between man and God. The host of the Holy Sacrament presents the direct objective presence of Christ. While for the Catholic, then, faith is bound to the invisible by visible objects of the Church, for Protestants faith tends to follow the accumulation of nonreligious objects provided by capitalistic enterprise.[23]

Opening the gates of the monastery to everyman effected a result similar to the inclusion of everyone within a monastic order. Protestant man became introspective, suppressed his former spontaneity, and strove for self-control. The consequence of this new life style for materialistic accumulation was spectacular, as Weber has shown. But of equal importance was the Protestant ethic's influence upon politics (which Weber did not demonstrate). Public activity came to be played with the same rationality, frugality, seriousness, and self-interestedness which Protestant man practiced in his religious and economic life. This was to be expected as the life of the "saved" was all of one cut—the ethic of Protestantism was unitary in nature. Only one city, the City of God, was worthy of Protestant man. And he strove to generalize his private religious values to all spheres of life.[24] Puritan New England became the embodiment of this world view—an attempt to align the public realm with Christian principle. As James Allen wrote in 1679 of the Puritans, "They came not hither to assert the prophetical or Priestly office of Christ so much, that were so fully owned in *Old England*, but . . . to bear witness to those truths concerning his visible Kingdome." [25]

This Protestant *zeitgeist* may be set in sharpest relief by comparing it with the Catholic ethical suppositions as set forth by Saint Thomas Aquinas. It is some thirteen centuries after Christianity's beginnings that defined place in Christian man's life. Aquinas, building upon the work the Earthly, namely, the public, sphere of action is given a significantly of Aristotle and Augustine, more approvingly and completely than anyone theretofore defined the possibilities of public action within a Christian commonwealth. He derived most of his religious premises from the thought of Saint Augustine.[26] Yet what he accomplishes is very different from Augustine, because Augustine, like the later Protestant movement, concerned himself primarily with man's relationship to the second city, the City of God. Saint Thomas, by contrast, devotes much of his work to the public sphere.

Aquinas, like Machiavelli who later built upon his thought, possessed an extremely practical bent. And Thomism was so successful in the late medieval era because it represented a set of premises which were congruent with the pattern of life of the time and fulfilled a recognized need. The life style of the thirteenth century was in many ways not "Christian"; it was in any case not a fellowship of love any more than was the post-Machiavellian modern period.[27] Accepting this situation, Aquinas institutionalizes access to the kingdom of heaven. From his time until the present, Catholics have been largely unconcerned·about their "election." Damnation only makes sense when man feels predestined, yet lacks the means to remedy the curse. Aquinas in restating the tenets of the Christian faith, firmly places the body of Christ, the *corpus christi*, under church control.[28] Through its monopoly upon the sacraments of baptism and of the Eucharist, the Church was able to dominate the tollgates leading to the City of God.

At this juncture in history, the Church becomes definitely equated with the City of God and the sociopolitical order identified with the Earthly City.[29] Clerical intermediaries between man and God could assure forgiveness of one's sins.[30] For those who came with penitence, absolution was possible.[31] As all men were seen as fallen, merely being "good" would never gain one's entrance into heaven. The sacraments of the Church were the keys to the kingdom, and these were accessible to all believers. While salvation was primarily a matter of God's grace and the sinner's faith, still, it was possible through human merit to supplement this precarious promise. The sacrifice of the Mass was accepted as such a meritorious work on the part of man, the sinner. The Creed of the Council of Trent summarizes this thought: "I acknowledge that the seven sacraments are: baptism, confirmation, Eucharist, penance, extreme unction, holy orders, and matrimony; and that *they confer grace.*" [32]

The problem of everyday religiosity for caudillaje man became unimportant while, simultaneously, periodic church attendance and participation in the Mass took on an overriding necessity. Once it is accepted that all men remain sinners, the fact of sin becomes less significant. Men grow equal in terms of their possibilities for salvation and afterlife. The Church could admit even the most wicked into its bosom. Routinized procedures for obtaining grace signify the norm. Mechanical exercises of a repetitive nature are then equated with religiosity. For example, Irish Catholics have available an official booklet entitled *How to Avoid Purgatory*. According to this work, those who say the little ejaculation, "Sacred Heart of Jesus, I place my trust in Thee," 100 times a day gain 30,000 days indulgence. Those who say it 1,000 times, each gain 300,000 days indulgence.

By contrast, Protestants divided the universe at the Reformation into the damned and the saved. The entire sociopolitical world was religionized by the individual's attempt to belong to the elect, or at least to give the appearance of election. Also, the assumption that one of God's elect could not be engaging in sin inevitably led Protestants to make sin *the* problem of the socioeconomic-political world.

For Catholics, at the precise moment that religious salvation became institutionalized, religiosity became unnecessary. It is for this reason that, speaking in terms of the Earthly City, a recent prelate of the Church could say of Latin America, "The vast majority of Catholics are *solo de nombre;* that is, nominal Catholics. . . . Though baptized and believing in the Catholic Faith, those nominal Catholics do not practice their religion or allow it to influence their daily lives in any appreciable degree." [33] With the paucity of the individual Catholic's moralistic fervor in everyday life, defense of the Church as a sacramental institution gains importance because it acts as a barrier between God's wrath and man's sin as well as an ever-present stepping-stone to salvation. This fact is obvious in caudillaje society where religiosity, among men at least, is rare, while anti-Catholic attitudes in the sense of denying the basic premises of the religion are even more rare.[34] One modern theologian has noted that the attempt to synthesize Christ with culture leads directly to the institutionalization of Christ and the Gospel.[35] This would appear to be as valid today in modern Latin America, for example, as it was in the Thomistic formulation of the thirteenth century. But, as we shall see, while religion became institutionalized, rigid, and unbending in Catholic Latin America, Italy, Spain, et al., politics became personalistic and heroic. It is interesting to compare the Protestant response to the world: religion became personal, and economics heroic, while politics became institutionalized—and to some extent rigid and inflexible.

But if Catholic men had become equal in the possibilities of afterlife, by what means could they be distinguished in the here-and-now? Denied even the dichotomous saved-damned predestination, few felt satisfied with a competition in piety. None of the Protestant smugness coterminous with the assurance that one belongs to the saved was possible, and therefore no reason afforded for competition in private excellence. Puritanism makes no sense when the impure can be similarly rewarded. The institutionalization of salvation and the guaranty of heavenly bliss for the common man forced Catholics to seek another basis for gaining deference and respect.

Saint Thomas resolved the dilemma by giving emphasis to the values of the city of classical times, that is, *public* values. This was made possible by his adoption of the Aristotelian division between the life of

action and the contemplative life, and by the superimposition of this
distinction upon the traditional Two Cities dichotomy of Augustine.
Saint Augustine's City of God is merged with the Aristotelian life of
contemplation; the Earthly City is united with the classical ideal of
the *vita activa*. New Testament Christianity was assigned to those who
were withdrawn from political life, while classicism was allotted to the
public man. The two realms had separate values. Aquinas, in building
his hierarchy, did not cancel the Augustinian distinction between good
and evil. Rather, he constitutionalized it. He recognized that ordinary
men cannot publicly abide by the ethical code of the City of God, but
that other, less ambitious values were necessary. These he found within
the writings of Aristotle. Aquinas's assimilation of Aristotle into the
Christian world was fortuitous in that it filled a void. This integration
provided general guidelines for men living in the *civitas terrena* where
previously no such norms had existed. It remained, however, for the
Renaissance to clarify these standards. Taking their cue from Saint
Thomas, "a group of thinkers arose who challenged the contempt with
which the medieval theologians regarded this world of ours and who
affirmed unequivocally that the earth was a goodly habitation and our
individual existence a most precarious gift." [36]

Unlike the later Protestants who shut themselves away in intro-
spection, loneliness, and a general realization of worldly asceticism in
pursuing their own salvation through private activity, Aquinas provided that Catholic man, once delivered from the need for actively
working out his own otherwordly destiny, could turn toward the
public. Henceforth, a Catholic, unlike a Protestant, need not impress the
public with his being of the elect in order to prove to *himself* that he
was saved. Rather, he could turn toward the pre-Christian, classical tradition for his ideas of immediate self-gratification and achievement.
Thus was accepted the premise of public action. In so doing, it was
boldly asserted that here in the Earthly City man could pursue his own
self-realization—a self-realization which had as its reward the applause
of the moment, of one's fellowmen, and of history. One *can* achieve a
certain immortality in the memory of a people or a nation. In short,
both the actions and the rewards of caudillaje man became primarily
secular and this-worldly.

In summary, the greatest achievement of the Middle Ages, the
institutionalization of Christianity, made unnecessary the "practice" of
religion by people of the Earthly City, the City of Man. Indeed, it did
more than that. It left a void of such major proportions that Western

man was forced to seek an entirely non-Christian set of this-worldly values in order to realize himself at the most basic level of his ego—or lose his own self-identity and reason for living in the banalities of animal existence.

It was the greatness of Aquinas that he recognized the Augustinian dichotomy for what it was—an existential abyss. In Aquinas's endeavor to integrate Aristotle with Christianity he perceived the need for, and carried forward, the classical secular value structure, a value structure oriented toward public activity that was eminently fitted for life in the medieval city. While, of course, Aquinas saw the scheme as one integrated whole reaching from heaven down to the humblest peasant, in fact, his introduction of pagan values as acceptable guidelines for worldly conduct meant that once the golden highway to heaven was cut by the bulldozers of man's cupidity—a force anticipated by Saint Augustine—the values of the Earthly City could return to a diluted classical base with precious little of Christianity remaining. Machiavelli became the almost inevitable consequence of Thomistic theology.

Thus the new ethic for the Earthly City was Catholic in its modern conception. But its roots were in the classical tradition. Above all, it was a secular ethos. It reflected the consequences of assuring one's salvation through institutionalized intermediaries and the use of indulgences. With the major problem of afterlife resolved, men turned toward their basic drive for self-realization; and both the rules and the rewards for this new City of Man were provided by Aquinas out of his study of Aristotle.

In modern Catholic societies, Aristotle has been played out to a perfectly logical, if not necessarily inevitable, conclusion. For one to say this is to presuppose that Saint Thomas classicized Christianity.[37] And in terms of the political implications of the philosophy of Aquinas, I believe this to be true. The Christian West by itself could never have arrived at the political entrepreneurship of Machiavelli. But through an early alignment of its values with the classical tradition, Renaissance dictatorship became possible. From the Italian *condottiere* of the fifteenth and sixteenth centuries to a culturewide caudillaje of the nineteenth and twentieth centuries was but a short step.

Christianity's concept of the Two Cities thus culminates in the thought of the Renaissance. Machiavelli became the last great theoretician within the traditional Catholic frame of reference.[38] His contribution was to complete the secularization of the City of Man.

The stage had been set for Machiavelli in the New Testament distinction between the things of Caesar and things of God. This early dichotomy had led to an emphasis upon man's private salvation and an eventual identification of man's soul with the Church as the depository and the means of salvation. Aquinas, in drawing upon the classics, gave an ethos to the public realm. This ethos was taken over by Machiavelli. What he did was largely to ignore the private man, the inner man, which Saint Thomas had preserved as central to his system. Machiavelli thus appropriated the ethic from the Middle Ages and from Aquinas (and Dante) as the spokesman of that age. (Friedrich Meinecke in his *Machiavellism: The Doctrine of Raison d'Etat and Its Place in Modern History*, represents a host of scholars who totally miss the dualism of medieval Christianity and Machiavelli's place within that tradition, when he suggests its beginnings in Machiavelli's writings: "The forces of sin, which had been basically subdued by the Christian ethic, now won what was fundamentally a partial victory; the devil forced his way into the kingdom of God. There now began that dualism under which modern culture has to suffer: that opposition between supra-empirical and empirical, between absolute and relative standards of value." [39] Just how wrong is Meinecke and this way of thinking becomes obvious when one recalls that Martin Luther, Machiavelli's contemporary, accepted the same Augustinian dualism: "We must divide all the children of Adam into two classes; the first belong to the kingdom of God, the second to the kingdom of the world." [40] Of importance, rather, is the fact that Machiavelli sought to help men find themselves within the Earthly City, while Luther attempted the same within the confines of the Heavenly City.) The classical values that Saint Thomas had introduced to govern men's actions in the Earthly City were now embraced with only minor attention given to one's relationship to the Church as a believer. Indeed Machiavelli was urging that, carried to its extreme, there was a public way of viewing the world so separated from man's private ethics or private virtue that one had to unlearn Christianity in order to practice it successfully. Man had to learn how "not to be good" within the public realm. Yet we know from reports upon his time that Westerners had internalized this lesson extremely well—Catholic man had, in fact, long since separated his private Christian side from his public activity. Thus, Machiavelli fulfilled the logic implicit in Christianity since its dualistic inception. He played out to its reductionistic conclusion the division of the world into two cities. For in Machiavelli we see all the possible consequences of a clear and distinct division of the world into two moralities, political or public and private or religious.

Machiavelli is such a striking figure in political philosophy because he articulated what everyone had known but had refrained from saying. He demonstrates what Augustine and Aquinas had suggested, that the ethics of the New Testament are not viable in a public setting. In Machiavelli's writings the thesis is only stated more boldly. As Ernesto Landi summarizes the matter, "Machiavelli argues that things which are rightly forbidden by private morality—violence, falsehood, the breaking of contracts, and so forth—are not only at times permitted but are at times demanded by political morality." [41] Machiavelli nowhere denies the validity of the Christian religion in the private sphere. He merely condemns its public side. He believes that the morality of the New Testament of love and humility is inappropriate to the political practice of men, primarily because men do not in fact live up to that ethic. "For love is held by a chain of obligation which, men being selfish, is broken whenever it serves their purpose." [42] In other words, corruption permeates the Earthly City, and this corruption will not be corrected by an appeal for individuals to act upon Christian principles. In fact, they have to learn the reverse.[43]

Christianity integrated with classicism led almost inevitably to Machiavelli and Machiavellianism. Machiavelli points out lucidly that the Church failed as a public restraint. He was acquainted with Savonarola, the corruption of popes and cardinals, and he saw that whatever the ethic did for man privately it did not curb or guide him publicly.[44] It is an interesting fact that those commentators who condemn Machiavelli, as well as those who see his political attitudes as being essentially neutral or nonmoral, admit that he took his examples from the Italian world at the time in which he lived.[45] He was stating the reality of a Catholic civilization in his "cruel work of exposure." [46] Specifically, Allan Gilbert has shown that Machiavelli derived most of his ideas from this recent historical past and not from the Roman setting which he often claimed to idolize.[47] Much the same would be said later about the origins of Simón Bolívar's indignant statements upon the nature of man; or Fidel Castro's allegedly historical (Marxist) "exposure" of North American imperialism.

It is the ethic of Augustine's Earthly City, the ethic of Aquinas's human law, the ethic finally of Machiavelli's prince, that we are summarizing. This ethic I have termed the Catholic ethic. While one may object to the inclusion of Machiavelli under the rubric of "Catholic," it should be stressed again that apart from the various logical and philosophical reasons which can be adduced, Machiavelli did live, write, and draw his contemporary examples primarily from the pre-Reformation era. However ugly the reality of his day, it was a "Catholic" reality. And Machiavelli was spokesman for that ambience. His uniqueness was to bring a singular focus upon the Earthly City. (That emphasis has been continued in the contemporary world by Catholic theorists. Two caudillaje writers, a Latin American and an Italian, in an adulatory work on President Stroessner of Paraguay, see nothing wrong, for example, in lumping together *"dos grandes pensadores:* Nicolas Maquiavelo *y* Jacques Maritain," as preeminent representatives of social theorizing. Laudably, theories of Machiavelli and Maritain provide the basis for Stroessner's rule, according to these authors.)[48]

As a man Machiavelli claims to be "more concerned with the salvation of his fatherland than with the salvation of his soul." [49] But this stance is a luxury that only one who embraces the Catholic ethos can maintain, for his soul reclines in the hands of the Church. It is of more than minor interest to find that Machiavelli himself received the last rites of the Church. According to a letter written by his son, Machiavelli "allowed fra Matteo to hear him confess his sins," and the friar stayed with him until his last breath.[50] Meinecke in his influential work on *raison d'état* performed a great disservice to scholarship by insisting upon the non-Christian nature of Machiavelli as a man: "It was therefore a historical necessity that the man, with whom the history of the idea of *raison d'état* in the modern Western world begins and from whom Machiavellism takes its name, had to be a heathen; he had to be a man to whom the fear of hell was unknown, and who on the contrary could set about his life-work of analyzing the essence of *raison d'état* with all the naivety of the ancient world." [51] All too many non-caudillaje scholars have been determined to make Machiavelli the scapegoat of the Western world by ignoring the sixteenth-century orthodoxy which he obviously embraced in his own life and articulated in his writings.[52] We also know that while living Machiavelli attended mass and used the language of traditional Christianity in his letters, and that he saw himself as "confirmed in grace." [53] In a striking passage in one of his letters, Machiavelli asserts his salvation while criticizing members of the clergy: "Your Lordship knows that these friars say that when one is confirmed in grace, the devil has no more power to tempt him. So I have no more fear that these friars will make me a hypocrite, because I believe I am very well confirmed." [54] The salvation of his soul being assured, Machiavelli was quite free to boast of his concern for the Earthly City, his fatherland. Protestants could not have stated that they loved anything more than their own souls precisely because they had no recourse to institutionalized salvation of the second city as embodied within the Church. As such, their ethos perennially remains aligned to the City of God; while it is the ethic of the Earthly City which has exerted such a profound influence upon peoples of the modern-day Catholic world.

Caudillaje civilization comes premised upon the classic Augustinian division between the City of Man and the City of God. We should ever beware of aligning the quest for personal power and glory with some temporary Marxist stage of economic development, on the one hand, or with a simplistic Renaissance "birth of evil" theory on the other. The first practitioners of the Catholic ethos in Latin America were not the leaders of the independence movement but the conquistadores, those contemporaries of Machiavelli who had learned the ethic in fifteenth-century Spain.[55] Their deeds now appear to us to contain duplicity. Yet, in retiring to mass before gloriously putting their hapless native adversaries to the sword, they were entirely consistent. The first act demonstrates a concern for private salvation, the second action would provide for one's public glory.[56] Great piety and great barbarism are alike possible within the confines of the concept of the Two Cities.[57] Catholics believed with Dante that "providence has set before man two ends to be pursued: namely, the beatitude of this life, which consists in the operation of his own virtue and is typified by the earthly paradise; and the beatitude of life eternal, which consists in the enjoyment of the divine countenance, to which man's own virtue cannot ascend unless it is aided by divine light; and this is described for our understanding as the heavenly paradise." [58]

Republican Latin America continued the Catholic ethical tradition. A division of the world into Two Cities had laid a foundation for the rise of caudillaje governance. Patriots of Latin America in searching for a viable alternative to the hegemony of Spanish colonialism fell back upon the only common denominator of their citizenry, the ethos of Catholicism. In so doing they conserved their past. This was only possible because they uniformly accepted dualistic Catholicism. Hidalgo, Morelos, San Martín, Moreno, Bolívar are representative in their agreement.[59] One cannot maintain that these leaders were devoted Catholics any more than one can contend that our constitutional founding fathers were devout Protestants. What is clear, however, is their acceptance of the Catholic ethical tradition as it had become secularized over the years. As integrated parts of a Catholic civilization, they had taken in these values with their mothers' milk. Those scholars who charge these men with Masonry and various other "liberal heresies" miss the point. As Weber noted concerning the Protestant ethic, once it was secularized its values were pervasive *regardless* of the religiosity of particular men. An interesting contemporary parallel can be seen in Latin American Protestants today who often appear to think and act like Catholics when they enter public life. In fact, Protestant churches in Latin America tend to be much more hierarchical, paternalistic, and authoritarian than their counterparts in Protestant-ethic countries. North Americans have invariably been oblivious to the theory of the Two Cities. Throughout social-science literature one finds continual laments over the apparent inadequacy of religious values to restrain caudillaje men within the public forum as occurs more or less successfully in Protestant-ethic countries. These culture biases simply fail to comprehend that caudillaje society neither expects nor allows the two spheres to overlap. Following is a typical Protestant-ethos-oriented lament: "The influence of the Church in the development of values, motivation, and behavior in Latin America is both obvious and disappointing in many ways. For the most part it has seemed that only a thin veneer of Christianity has been developed rather than any real appreciation or respect for man, his rights and dignity." [60]

Agreement upon dualistic Catholicism opens the way to a de facto separation between religion and everyday life throughout caudillaje culture. Whether Church and State are officially united, caudillaje man believes with Simón Bolívar that "religion has no bearing upon... [political and civil] rights, it is by nature indefinable in the social organization, because it lies in the moral and intellectual sphere. Religion governs man in his home, within his own walls, within himself.... Laws, on the contrary, deal with surface things; they are applicable outside the home of a citizen." [61] Applied in the contemporary world, the Cuban revolution furnishes an example. Castro in a speech states: "The same respect that the Revolution ought to have for religious beliefs, ought those who talk in the name of religion also to have for the political beliefs of others. And, above all, to have present that which Christ said: 'My kingdom is not of this world.' (Applause.) What are those who are said to be the interpreters of Christian thought doing meddling in the problems of this world?" [62]

Here in the language of the early nineteenth and mid-twentieth centuries are lucid statements of Machiavelli's position. Caudillaje invariably followed upon this accepted separation between private and public morality.[63] And it lives on today throughout the Catholic world.

NOTES

CHAPTER I

1. On Weber's use of the term, see Herbert Luethy, "Once Again: Calvinism and Capitalism," in Dennis Wrong, ed., *Max Weber* (Englewood Cliffs, N.J.: Prentice-Hall, 1970), pp. 127ff.
2. R. H. Tawney, in a preface to the 1936 edition of his celebrated *Religion and the Rise of Capitalism* (London: John Murray), notes that when his work first appeared it was possible for a reviewer to dispute his use of the term *capitalism* as being none other than a political catchword (p. xi).
3. For example, Seymour Lipset exhibits this kind of prejudice when he says: "The high prestige of the university in Latin America is to some extent linked to its identification with the elite, with the assumption that professors and graduates, 'doctors,' are gentlemen. However, such an identity is not dependent on the universities' contribution to society, and is clearly dysfunctional in any society which seeks to develop economically, or to make contributions to the world of science and scholarship." "Values, Education, and Entrepreneurship," in Seymour Lipset and Aldo Solari, eds., *Elites in Latin America* (New York: Oxford University Press, 1967), p. 22. Elsewhere he says that the predominant values of Latin America "are in large measure antithetical to rational entrepreneurial orientations" (p. 28).
4. "El que, como cabeza y superior, guía y manda a la gente." The *Diccionario manueal e ilustrado de la lengua española* (1950) defines a caudillo as "el que dirige algún gremio, comunidad o cuerpo." The word *caudillaje* is not entirely new to discussions of social behavior. Heretofore, however, its use appears to have been restricted to the political sphere. See, for example, Fernando N. A. Cuevillas, "El régimen del caudillaje en Hispanoamérica," *Boletín del Instituto de Sociología* 11 (1953): 59–75.
5. A derivative of the Italian word *condottiere* might have been used. Interestingly, Che Guevara called himself not a caudillo but a "little twentieth-century condottiere." *Venceremos! The Speeches and Writings of Ernesto Che Guevara*, ed. John Gerassi (New York: Simon & Schuster, 1968), p. 412.

6. Values are assumed in this study to be general orientations toward basic aspects of life; that is, abstract concepts, or principles that guide behavior. See Clyde Kluckhohn, "Value and Value-Orientations in the Theory of Action," in Talcott Parsons and Edward A. Shils, eds., *Toward a General Theory of Action* (Cambridge: Harvard University Press, 1954), pp. 388–433.

7. Leopoldo Zea and a myriad of social theorists, especially novelists, have suggested that "everyman" tends to live vicariously through a "larger" personality. While many will say this fact qualifies my theory significantly, I do not believe that to be the case. Rather, one sees in such attachment the power of a strong personality to attract; and tacit recognition by the follower that he cannot compete—but this truth hardly alters the competitive approach to life of the individual. He will compete publicly with others. In fact, his attachment to a great *patrón* who can assist him in time of need provides the *raison d'être* for such an alliance.

8. Eric R. Wolf and Edward Hansen, "Caudillo Politics: A Structural Analysis," *Comparative Studies in Society and History* 9, no. 2 (1967): 168–79, for example, relate caudillaje exclusively to the nineteenth century. Here I am taking issue with those who see caudillaje society as crosscut with diverse value systems. Except insofar as the following statement relates to isolated Indian settlements, I believe it is mistaken. Those who look for diversity will find it, but those who look for unifying themes will find them also. In any case, T. Lynn Smith maintains that "the first fact to be kept constantly in mind is the tremendous variation to be encountered with respect to the values held by those with whom we will deal in various parts of Latin America." *Studies of Latin American Societies* (Garden City, N.Y.: Doubleday Anchor, 1970), p. 247. Strangely enough, Smith on the previous page sees North Americans as wearing "a particular type of 'spectacles' through which we interpret the world." Yet in Latin America, with a culture which is more monolithic in terms of origin, language, and religion, he wants to see only diversity!

9. Oscar Lewis was an astute reporter of Latin American mores. But he, and those who followed him, performed a disservice to cultural understanding by attempting to explain behavior of the poor as tied to a "culture of poverty" rather than the larger culture in which they lived, albeit certain similarities do exist among the behavior of the poor—as Lewis maintained—or among the behavior of the rich—as Karl Marx maintained. For a perceptive, if overstated, attack on Lewis's theory, see Anthony Leeds, "The Concept of the 'Culture of Poverty': Conceptual, Logical, and Empirical Problems, with Perspectives from Brazil and Peru," in Eleanor Burke Leacock, *The Culture of Poverty* (New York: Simon & Schuster, 1971), pp. 226–84.

10. On the relationship between leaders and followers, see James C. Davies, *Human Nature and Politics* (New York: John Wiley, 1963), chap. 9; and Herbert McClosky et al., "Issue Conflict and Consensus among Party Leaders and Followers," in Edgar Litt, *The Political Imagination* (Glenview, Ill.: Scott, Foresman & Co., 1966), pp. 223–56.

One of the shakiest theories regarding Latin America has had to do with the emergence of a middle class in some of these nations. What is belatedly being asked is whether the middle class in fact possesses a different world view that sets it apart from the older caudillaje culture. In other words, does this class have egalitarian, liberal democratic, and capitalistic values? Charles Wagley, *The Latin American Tradition* (New York: Columbia University Press, 1968), pp. 21–22, notes: "These criteria certainly show the varied strength of a middle strata in the various nations, but there is still some doubt whether such groups are, in fact, set off from others in their nations by cultural criteria—by a distinctive ideology, behavior patterns and self-identity."

Richard N. Adams has also been perceptive in this regard. See his "Political Power and Social Structure," in Claudio Véliz, ed., *The Politics of Conformity in Latin America* (London: Oxford University Press, 1967), pp. 15–42. I believe Adams's adoption of the Marxist two-class analysis is helpful in correcting former erroneous ideas concerning the growth and implications of a middle class in Latin America. Yet, I think he does not go far enough to recognize that many upper-class values are culturewide. If one looks one will find most upper-class values also present in the lower class.

11. Cited by Herbert Matthews, *Fidel Castro* (New York: Simon & Schuster, 1970), p. 15.

12. Ramón Menéndez Pidal, *The Spaniards in Their History*, trans. Walter Starkie (New York: Norton Library, 1966), p. 21. "It has always been a great quality as well as a great defect of the Spaniard to allow himself to be swayed by idealistic motives rather than by the desire for economic profit" (p. 20).

13. Éléna de la Souchère, *An Explanation of Spain, trans.* Eleanor R. Levieux (New York: Random House, 1964), p. 76. "The Spanish masses are curiously indifferent to politics" (p. 338). The lengths to which villagers may go in avoiding public office has been sketched by Erich Fromm and Michael Maccoby, *Social Character in a Mexican Village* (Englewood Cliffs, N.J.: Prentice-Hall, 1970), p. 209.

14. Fidel Castro is well within the tradition we are describing with his axiom, *La jefatura es básica* ("Leadership is basic"). Theodore Draper argues correctly that this axiom is "far more closely related to 'leadership principle' movements such as fascism and Peronism than to an ideology-and-party-conscious movement such as Communism." *Castroism: Theory and Practice* (New York: Praeger, 1965), p. 9.

15. V. S. Pritchett, *Dublin: A Portrait* (New York: Harper & Row, 1967), p. 74.

16. V. S. Pritchett, *The Spanish Temper* (New York: Harper & Row, 1965), pp. 10–11. References to culturewide elitism abound. See, for example, Jesse R. Pitts, "Continuity and Change in Bourgeois France," in Stanley Hoffmann et al., *In Search of France* (Cambridge: Harvard University Press, 1963), p. 236: "The aristocracy and the bourgeoisie, of course, make up only a small fraction of the French population, perhaps 3 or 4 percent Their great importance resides in their having provided a model for those below them in the social hierarchy." Richard A. Barrett, *Benabarre: The Modernization of a Spanish Village* (New York: Holt, Rinehart, & Winston, 1974), pp. 26ff., uses the term "gentleman complex" to denote this attitude. "The term 'gentleman complex' refers to the fact that, in attitudes toward work and leisure, Benabarre's elite pursued a quasi-aristocratic ideal," says Barrett. "It should be understood, however, that the complex applied in varying degrees to all segments of prewar society; and, furthermore, remains influential in contemporary Spain" (p. 27). Menéndez Pidal, *Spaniards in Their History*, pp. 29–30, also emphasizes the

point. The extensive nature of this elitism can be surmised from Oscar Lewis's recording of the words of Manuel Sánchez, a lower-class Mexican: "Instead of trying to raise a person's morale, our motto here is, 'If I am a worm, I'm going to make the next fellow feel like a louse.' Yes, here you always have to feel you are above. I have felt this way myself, that's why I say it. I guess I'm a Mexican, all right. Even if you live on the bottom level, you have to feel higher up. I've seen it among the trash pickers; there's rank even among thieves. They start arguing, 'You so-and-so, all you steal is old shoes. But me, when I rob, I rob good stuff.' So the other one says, 'You! Turpentine is all you drink. At least, I knock off my 96-proof pure alcohol, which is more than you ever do.' That's the way things are here." *The Children of Sánchez* (New York: Vintage Books, 1961), p. 339.

Social scientists have often mentioned the elitist ethos within contemporary society. Relevant are Wagley's observations regarding the culturewide nature of Hispanic values: "The aristocratic ideal patterns inherited from Spain and Portugal and cultivated in the New World filtered down to all sectors of the Latin American population, except perhaps the most isolated Indian communities." *Latin American Tradition*, p. 5. In noting that the elitist ideals were taken over by the peasantry in Latin America, Wagley remarks that the Latin American culture patterns "are aristocratic patterns and derivative of the gentry" (p. 4).

Concerning the middle class, Bernard J. Siegel comments on Brazil: "Rather than considering themselves a new 'middle class,' these newly successful groups have come to share, with the descendants of the old landed gentry, an aristocratic set of ideals and patterns of behavior which they have inherited from the nobility of the Brazilian empire." "Social Structure and Economic Change in Brazil," in Simon Kuznets, Wilbert E. Moore, and Joseph J. Spengler, eds., *Economic Growth: Brazil, India, Japan* (Durham, N.C.: Duke University Press, 1955), pp. 405–6.

17. Joseph Aceves, *Social Change in a Spanish Village* (London: Schenkman, 1971), p. 68.
18. *The Protestant Ethic and the Spirit of Capitalism* (New York: Scribner's, 1958), p. 117.
19. Ibid., pp. 58–59.
20. As a matter of fact, Weber's own analysis of Hinduism unfortunately pursued a teleological course by seeking out the irrational (retarding) influence of Hinduism upon the development of capitalism in India. "It was impossible to shatter traditionalism, based on caste ritualism anchored in *karma* doctrine, by rationalizing the economy," he said. And, on the other hand, "the effects of the caste system on the economy . . . were essentially negative . . . . This order by its nature is completely traditionalistic and anti-rational in its effects." Max Weber, *The Religion of India: The Sociology of Hinduism and Buddhism* (New York: Free Press, 1958), pp. 123, 111. For an astute comparison of Weber's treatment of Europe with his treatment of India, see Milton Singer, *When a Great Tradition Modernizes* (New York: Praeger, 1972), pp. 277–82.
21. Weber, *Protestant Ethic*, p. 60.
22. A contemporary application of this mistaken Weberian notion of rationality can be found in Norman E. Whitten, "Power, Structure and Sociocultural

Change in Latin American Communities," in Arpad von Lazar and Robert R. Kaufman, eds., *Reform and Revolution: Readings in Latin American Politics* (Boston: Allyn & Bacon, 1969), pp. 249–66. Misuse of rationality leads Whitten to the culture-bound *ad hominem* statement that "the caudillo pattern usurps a rational structure to further unsanctioned, personal power" (p. 258). Such a view is not surprising given his definition of *rational*. "*Rational* refers to the systematic centralized arrangement, secularization, and impersonalization of the ability to influence activities" (p. 250). By contrast, the argument of this book is that personalization of life can be an extremely rational form of behavior.

An unfortunate result of some social scientists' thinking has been the all-too-common tendency to equate rationality with economically developed nations and to place all other countries in one category, refusing to pay heed to cultural variations. Thus we get such misleading statements as "Latin America's political problems are common to all developing countries"; or "the danger of the president's becoming a dictator looms very large in Latin America, but it does not derive from his broad powers. In developing countries this type of regime could not function properly in any other way." Jacques Lambert, *Latin America: Social Structure and Political Institutions* (Berkeley: University of California Press, 1967), pp. 49, 19. On such assumptions as these have we built and endeavored to implement theories of development around the world during the past twenty years—results both academic and policywise have not been impressive.

One astute essay on the traditional-modern dichotomy is that by John M. Brewster, "Beliefs, Values, and Economic Development," *American Journal of Agricultural Economics* 43 (1961): 779–96.

23. Manuel Sánchez, in Lewis, *Children of Sánchez*, p. 349. In modern Poland the value frame appears to be similar: "The habits of economy and living on a budget are not well developed in the home, frugality, industry, and the amassing of wealth are not particularly valued, and the future is rarely viewed in concrete terms." Clifford R. Barnett, *Poland, Its People, Its Society, Its Culture* (New Haven: HRAF Press, 1958), p. 407.

Personal aspirations of a people are, of course, related to national goals. Simón Bolívar, the liberator of South America, states the capitalistic-caudillaje cleavage well by defining his goals: "I desire to see America fashioned into the greatest nation in the world, greatest not so much by virtue of her area and wealth as by her freedom and glory." *Selected Writings of Bolívar* (New York: Colonial Press, 1951), p. 115. Given this tradition one should not be surprised by Fidel Castro's antimonetary views; for Castro represents caudillaje society by his general aversion to accumulation of material wealth for its own sake. Herbert Matthews has observed that "Fidel's contempt for money went so far that when he first came to power in 1959, he even grumbled because banks were charging interest. This was not only a throwback to medieval Catholic doctrine about the evils of 'usury'; it was also one of the many ways in which Fidel's ideas resembled some of the pre-Marxist schools of socialism and modern anarchism. It is this anti-money instinct that inclines him—as it did Che Guevara—to feel that the rewards of labor should be moral rather than materialistic." Matthews, *Fidel Castro*, p. 35.

24. Víctor Raúl Haya de la Torre, *¿A dónde va Indoamérica?* (Santiago, Chile: Editorial Ercilla, 1935), p. 25.
25. Charles L. Sanford, ed., *Benjamin Franklin and the American Character* (Boston: D. C. Heath, 1955), p. 11.
26. Niccolò Machiavelli, *Il principe e discorsi* (Milan: Gianiacomo Feltrinelli Editore, 1960), p. 27.
27. My general view of power corresponds to that of Carl J. Friedrich: "Power can best be described in terms of followership." *An Introduction to Political Theory* (New York: Harper & Row, 1967), p. 123.
28. Karl W. Deutsch, *The Nerves of Government* (New York: Free Press, 1966), pp. 120–21; emphasis mine.
29. David C. McClelland and David G. Winter, *Motivating Economic Achievement* (New York: Free Press, 1969), p. 61. In an earlier work McClelland states his thesis simply: "It was not anticipated that *n* Power would be related to economic development, nor in fact did it turn out to be." *The Achieving Society* (Princeton, N.J.: Van Nostrand, 1961), p. 168.

    McClelland's studies and those growing out of his work have noted the classlessness of cultural differences—a theme that I shall insist upon in this work. For example, in a comparative study of economic achievement values of Brazilian and North American students, it was found that "Brazilian boys on the average have lower achievement motivation than their American peers . . . [that] upper, middle, and lower class Brazilians tend to have lower achievement motivation scores than Americans of a comparable class. *What is more startling is the finding that the mean score of Brazilian boys in any social class is lower than the motivation score of Americans . . . whatever their class may be*." Bernard Rosen, "The Achievement Syndrome and Economic Growth in Brazil," *Social Forces* 42 (1964): 345–46; Rosen's emphasis.
30. Machiavelli, *Il principe*, chaps. 6, 8, 12.
31. *The Second Treatise of Civil Government*, chapter 5, pars. 46–48. One can see the different orientations of two cultures even in the *method* utilized for studying natural phenomenon. According to Prof. Gene Martin, Latin American geography textbooks emphasize *political* units while geography texts written within the United States tend to focus much more heavily upon *economic* products.
32. For an example of a Parsonian approach to Spanish society, see the essays by Amando de Miguel in issues of the *Revista del Instituto de la Juventud* (August 1965 through August 1966). De Miguel uses the concept *amiguismo* or "friendism" to characterize Spanish behavior and life. Seymour Lipset develops some of the implications for Parsons's pattern variables in Latin America. See "Values, Education, and Entrepreneurship," pp. 5–8.
33. In his association with the Sánchez family in Mexico, Oscar Lewis, a "Lockean" anthropologist, was appropriately "struck by the absence of monetary motivation in their relationship with me. Basically, it was their sense of friendship that led them to tell me their life stories." *Children of Sánchez*, p. xx. Alexander J. Humphreys, *New Dubliners: Urbanization and the Irish Family* (New York: Fordham University Press, 1966), pp. 15–17, discusses the concept of "friendliness" among the Irish. He concludes that friendliness "is much more important and powerful in the rural community than class considera-

tions" (p. 17). Donald S. Connery, *The Irish* (New York: Simon & Schuster, 1968), p. 92, notes that in Ireland "personal networks of friends and acquaintances are especially large."

34. Herbert W. Schneider, ed., *Adam Smith's Moral and Political Philosophy* (New York: Hafner, 1948), p. 231. Ben Franklin's homilies coincided with Smith's later moralisms. For example, Smith, as noted above, feared the corrupting effects of gatherings marked by the "gayety of their conversation," while Franklin in his "Advice to Youth" of 1749, urged men "in converse be reserved, yet not morose." Nathan G. Goodman, ed., *A Benjamin Franklin Reader* (New York: Crowell, 1945), p. 279.

35. Lewis, *Children of Sánchez*, p. 171; emphasis mine. Pritchett writes of Spain: "If time *is* an object, if it *is* a matter of life and death, then a black figure which all Spaniards understand, rises up and interposes her immovable hand —the great croupier, Fate. '*Ay, señor, que triste es la vida.*'" *Spanish Temper*, p. 17.

36. Lewis, *Children of Sánchez*, p. 171. Cf. p. 424.

37. Ibid.; emphasis mine. Elsewhere, Jesús Sánchez reinforces the idea: "It's good to be thrifty, but you shouldn't go too far. Too much of anything is harmful" (p. 483). In another of his books, *La vida* (New York: Vintage, 1965), p. 27, Oscar Lewis records the words of Fernanda, a lower-class Puerto Rican: "I've made lots of money and I've spent it all. What would I want to keep it for? We're not made of stone and we all must die, right? Suppose I save money in the bank and then I die. Who is going to enjoy that money? The government! No, I'd rather eat up my money myself before they come and take care of it for me."

38. Translated by Eric Mosbacher as *The House by the Medlar Tree* (New York: Grove Press, 1953), p. 58.

39. On the wide meaning of *friend* in Ireland, see Conrad M. Arensberg, *Family and Community in Ireland* (Cambridge: Harvard University Press, 1968), pp. 72–75. Nonutilitarian friendship does, however, have a long and honored tradition within caudillaje society. José Martí, for example, wrote: "Love has not, to my recollection, given me any supreme moment; friendship has." Richard B. Gray, *José Martí, Cuban Patriot* (Gainesville: University of Florida Press, 1962), p. 39. "If they ask me what word is most beautiful, I will say that it is 'country'; and if they ask me for another, almost as beautiful as 'country,' I will say 'friendship'" (ibid.).

40. It is this fact that lies behind the common saying within caudillaje society, "There are as many political parties as there are voters." Gordon Di Renzo, *Personality, Power, and Politics* (Notre Dame, Ind.: University of Notre Dame Press, 1967), p. 58. An indication of the substance of that expression in Italy can be seen in the fact that prior to the 1963 election, over seventy parties applied for registration in the Rome electoral district alone. Irving R. Levine, *Main Street Italy* (New York: Doubleday, 1963), p. 116. On Spain, see Fernando Díaz-Plaja, *El español y los siete pecados capitales* (Madrid: Alianza Editorial, 1966), pp. 69–70. John McCarthy, *The Home Book of Irish Humor* (New York: Dodd, Mead, 1968), pp. 58ff., claims that the Irish are "Born Politicos."

The Mafia—that most Catholic and caudillaje organization—also utilizes friendship as a weapon of power. Mario Puzo in *The Godfather* (Greenwich, Conn.: Fawcett, 1969), p. 294, portraying a meeting of the chiefs, says: "The other Dons in the room applauded and rose to shake hands with everybody in sight and to congratulate Don Corleone and Don Tattaglia on their new friendship. It was not perhaps the warmest friendship in the world, they would not send each other Christmas gift greetings, but they would not murder each other. That was friendship enough in this world, all that was needed." Elsewhere the Godfather chastises his godson with these words: "Friendship is everything. Friendship is more than talent. It is more than government. It is almost the equal of family. Never forget that. If you had built up a wall of friendships you wouldn't have to ask me to help" (p. 38). That Puzo in no way exaggerates has been borne out by available evidence. E. J. Hobsbawm in *Social Bandits and Primitive Rebels* (Glencoe, Ill.: Free Press, 1959), pp. 34-35, writes, for example, that "once initiated the *Mafioso* was a *compadre*, cogodparenthood being in Sicily, as elsewhere in the Mediterranean, the form of artificial kinship which implied the greatest and most solemn obligations of mutual help on the contracting parties." In French Canada the civil service has been likened unto a mafia. Before 1960 in Quebec the government was run "as if it were a family business." When someone had a problem he simply "picked up the phone and called a friend." Peter Desbarats, *The State of Quebec* (Montreal: McClelland & Stewart, 1965), p. 109.

In Spain, says Menéndez Pidal, *Spaniards in Their History*, pp. 49-50, "Caciquism or the petty-boss system organized the most shameless illegality under the motto: 'Go as far as injustice for your friend and refuse justice to your enemy' (*Al amigo hasta lo injusto, y al enemigo ni lo justo*)." A comparatively recent account of the power of friendship can be seen in José Varallanos, *El cholo y el Peru* (Buenos Aires: Imprenta López, 1962), pp. 216-24.

41. John Santos, "Personal Values," in Samuel Shapiro, ed., *Integration of Man and Society in Latin America* (Notre Dame, Ind.: University of Notre Dame Press, 1967), p. 7, has used the phrase, "playing the friendship game."

42. From an interview cited in Frank Bonilla, *The Failure of Elites* (Cambridge: MIT Press, 1970), pp. 127-31.

43. McClelland, *Achieving Society*, shows that affiliation, which he defines as "friendship" (p. 160), is negatively related to need for Achievement (p. 166): *n*Achievement in turn he relates to economic achievement (p. 63). One must grant, however, that the easiest method for acquiring "friends" is economic well-being. François Chevalier's observations upon the Latin American colonial period still ring true today: "There were few obstacles for the private citizens who had the means, whether Spaniard, crioles, or mestizo, to have permanently the kind of personal following that poverty, insecurity, or the hostility of the environment often rendered natural." " 'Caudillos' et 'caciques' en Amérique: contribution à l'étude des liens personnels," reprinted in Hugh M. Hamill, ed., *Dictatorship in Spanish America* (New York: Knopf, 1965), p. 38.

44. J. A. Pitt-Rivers, *The People of the Sierra* (Chicago: University of Chicago Press, 1961), p. 140.

45. Luigi Barzini, *The Italians* (New York: Bantam Books, 1965), p. 238. A typical Spanish example of the surrounded man is recorded by Stanley G. Payne,

Falange: A History of Spanish Fascism (Stanford: Stanford University Press, 1961), p. 83. Head of the Falange until his execution in 1936, Primo de Rivera built his following. "José Antonio's worst defect as a party leader was his difficulty in choosing capable subordinates. A sycophantic camarilla grew up around him in Madrid, composed of old personal friends, fascistic poets, his former law clerks, and other flatterers. The *Jefe* was far too indulgent in his personal relationships to maintain the coldly objective attitude required of a political leader."

46. "Villagers assume that every man is surrounded by a large network of bilateral relatives, compadres, and friends. Success in village politics depends upon such resources." Cynthia Nelson, *The Waiting Village: Social Change in Rural Mexico* (Boston: Little, Brown, 1971), p. 87.

47. Mary N. Díaz, *Tonalá: Conservatism, Responsibility, and Authority in a Mexican Town* (Berkeley: University of California Press, 1970), pp. 44–45. "It must be impossible to be alone in Dublin. The Irish ... hate to be alone!" H. V. Morton, *In Search of Ireland* (New York: Dodd, Mead, 1946), p. 10.

48. Taylor sketches the Roman reality of Cicero. "At his house in Rome, which, Cicero emphasizes, should be a seemly mansion, with plenty of space in it, he had to be ready in the morning to greet the family clients and retainers and friends who came for the daily *salutatio*, and in the Forum he had to appear with a retinue and to be always at the call of any friend who might need him in the courts." Lily R. Taylor, *Party Politics in the Age of Caesar* (Berkeley: University of California Press, 1964), p. 30.

49. Miguel Angel Asturias, *El señor presidente* (New York: Atheneum, 1975), p. 97.

50. Allowing for a bit of overstatement, the following portrays with some validity the behavior of caudillaje man as opposed to capitalistic man. "The strength of the United States is in the community, not in the individual; the best of Mexico is in the individual person, not in the social being. This is the reason why the North American appears in an unfavorable light when he is detached from his group and is seen as an individual, as he must be seen, perforce, abroad. Rarely will he seem distinguished, that is to say different. Almost always he appears vulgar.

"The Mexican, on the other hand, will appear distinguished, different, or individual, not only in the color of his skin but in the tone of his voice and his calm, deliberate manner." Daniel Cosi Villegas, *American Extremes*, trans. Américo Paredes (Austin: University of Texas Press, 1964), p. 49.

51. Barzini, *The Italians*, p. 119. By systemic, then, one is implying that a plan or course of action guides behavior. The shrewdness of an Italian woman in search of a particular mate can follow this approach. "All of this may seem a great ado about a common dilemma of the young in love—except that Cettina was not 'in love': she had found her *sistemazione* for life. She did not suffer, or pine, or yearn for Vittorio, but she did all those things for his station in life. She was trying to capture a lifetime job and would have admitted, had she been asked, that little or no emotion was involved, knowing that any woman would understand and approve. Such calculations are the assumptions of a Southern woman's life." Ann Cornelisen, *Women of the Shadows* (Boston: Little, Brown, 1976), p. 173.

52. A. L. Maraspini, *The Study of an Italian Village* (Paris: Mouton, 1968), pp. 152–53, 158.

53. Joseph Lopreato, *Peasants No More: Social Class and Social Change in an Underdeveloped Society* (San Francisco: Chandler, 1967), p. 84, reports on an Italian émigré who had returned to his country after living in Australia. He marveled at the Australian lack of long waiting and the absence of a preferential service system. "Here," he said, "it is first-come-last-served, unless you come accompanied by a *commendatore* (honorific title)." He then goes on to describe his long hours of waiting day after day in order to see an official. This explains Almond and Verba's table demonstrating Mexican and Italian low expectation of equal treatment or consideration by government or police. Gabriel Almond and Sidney Verba, *The Civic Culture* (Princeton: Princeton University Press, 1963), p. 112.

54. Ann Cornelisen, *Torregreca: Life, Death, Miracles* (New York: Dell, 1969), p. 169.

55. R. N. Adams, *The Second Sowing* (San Francisco: Chandler, 1967), pp. 179–80. Pritchett, *Spanish Temper*, p. 93, notes that "Spanish writers used to attack their rulers for being so public and available and having no regard for the reserves of office."

56. Barzini, *The Italians*, pp. 66–67.

57. Ibid., p. 71.

58. Ibid., p. 83.

59. Nelson, *Waiting Village*, p. 53, says that in a Mexican town "the introduction of capital alone does not effect any basic change because increased capital does not alter the basic pattern of social relations or the values that support these relations."

60. La Souchère, *Explanation of Spain*, p. 344.

61. Gavin Maxwell, *The Ten Pains of Death* (New York: E. P. Dutton, 1960), p. 122.

62. In a study made of how the people of Caracas spend their free time, three types of action-oriented activity were included in the questionnaire: (1) going to church; (2) visiting friends; and (3) attending meetings of unions, clubs, religious meetings, political parties, etc. Every group except the *religiosos* most frequently visited friends. For most this appeared to be their major activity. Comision Nacional del Cuatricentenario de Caracas, *Cómo utilizan los caraqueños el tiempo libre* (Caracas: Editorial Sucre, 1966), pp. 65–70.

   The family, of course, constitutes the first line of friends. Aubrey Menen, "The Italian Family Is a Commune," *New York Times Magazine*, March 1, 1970, pp. 22ff., convincingly demonstrates this point.

63. Horace Miner, *St. Denis: A French-Canadian Parish* (Chicago: University of Chicago Press, 1963), p. 99. There is a bit of irony in the fact that within the convents of religious orders the same need for personal influence exists. A member of the Sisters of Misericordia states her feelings: "I'm a nun, but I feel I have the quality to be a Mother Superior—I know very well I have! Our Mother Superior is getting rather old, and she's not really suited to the work. Perhaps it'll be me who takes her place, or perhaps some other nun, depending on where the Mother General's sympathies lie. Everything's a question of the Party and of recommendation—I know a lot of important

people, even the bishop himself, and one day, God willing, I too shall be able
to glory in being a Mother Superior."

64. Maxwell, *Ten Pains of Death*, p. 181. Dionisio Ridruejo, *Escrito en España*
(Buenos Aires: Lasada, 1962), p. 135. In Italy, "no matter what his qualifications, real or certified, [one] knows there is no hope without recommenda-
tions. If a friend of the sister-in-law of his wife's second cousin married a
Deputy's chauffeur, then he can maneuver for a testimonial that will carry
some weight, but if he has no such close tie, he must count on numbers to
make up for quality. In this treasure hunt almost any man who wears a white
shirt and black shoes and almost any woman in kid pumps who carries a
leather purse is a possible asset. They can, at least, write, and they might even
have connections." Cornelisen, *Women of the Shadows*, p. 68.

65. Maraspini, *Italian Village*, pp. 111–12.

66. Ibid., p. 112.

67. Arensberg has shown lucidly the interchangeability of words categorizing
"friend" and "relative" in Ireland. Conrad M. Arensberg, *Irish Countryman*
(Gloucester, Mass.: Peter Smith, 1959), pp. 66–69. Barzini writes, "everybody's
status, security, and welfare, depend on power. The first source of power is
the family. The strength of the family is determined by many factors—wealth,
connections, alliances, prestige, rank, luck—but, above all, by its inner cohe-
sion and ramifications." *The Italians*, pp. 210–11. John Gillin, "Ethos Components in Modern Latin American Culture," in Dwight B. Heath and Richard
N. Adams, eds., *Contemporary Cultures and Societies of Latin America* (New
York: Random House, 1965), p. 510, lists various means of friendship aggregation in Latin America. "Now, in Latin American culture there are three
pathways or patterns whereby one may establish intimate-friendship relations
with other persons in this sense: (1) kinship, including both consanguineal
and affinal (the latter somewhat weaker than the former); (2) ceremonial
friendship or 'kinship,' which so far as the *compadrazgo* is concerned is actually a formalized or institutionalized form of friendship...; (3) and 'mere
pure friendship' (*mera pura amistad*) which in many cases is established
between individuals who understand each other's souls, but who do not think
of imposing on each other by invoking the relationship of *compadrazgo*. In
the latter case, once the relationship is established, the persons involved address each other in the '*tu*' form (*vos*, in some parts) and enjoy certain joking
privileges with each other not permitted to those in a more formal relationship. Friendship, or the intimate personal connection, is the essential of interpersonal relations in the Latin American culture" (p. 510).

68. Mexican villagers were asked by an anthropologist to respond orally to the
picture of a little boy in a doorway. The researcher concluded: "Erongaricuarenos are preoccupied with the fear of separation and loneliness. All thirty
villagers included among their responses stories about a child being left un-
supported by his parents or orphaned, or a person being abandoned and need-
ing someone to take care of him." Nelson, *Waiting Village*, p. 112. Also see,
for example, comments in Lewis, *Children of Sánchez*, pp. 248, 482.

69. On the importance of the family, see especially Wagley, *Latin American Tradition*, p. 6. Within businesses in Latin America, for example, "managers are
frequently selected on the basis of family links rather than specialized train-

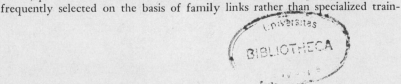

ing." Albert Lauterback, "Government and Development: Managerial Attitudes in Latin America," *Journal of Inter-American Studies* 4 (1962): 322. On the family enterprise in Latin America, see Lipset, "Values, Education, and Entrepreneurship," pp. 13–17; Adams, *Second Sowing,* pp. 60, 157, 159; Thomas C. Cochran and Rubén Reina, *Entrepreneurship in Argentine Culture* (Philadelphia: University of Pennsylvania Press, 1962); John J. Johnson, ed., *Continuity and Change in Latin America* (Stanford: Stanford University Press, 1964), pp. 161–85.

70. That the system of the extended family may become altered by time and circumstances, however, can be seen in the "amoral familism" described by Edward C. Banfield, *The Moral Basis of a Backward Society* (New York: Free Press, 1958).

71. The lack of a frontier spirit in Latin America since the conquest can probably be largely attributed to a reticence on the part of individuals to leave their extended family with its overlapping connections. It would be like facing the Latin American bureaucratic social-economic-political structure without "friends"—a frightening thing. The same consideration has probably slowed the already very rapid migration of peoples to the cities in the past decade. One author has noted this same lack of a frontier spirit in French Canada. Desbarats, *State of Quebec,* p. 2.

72. Santos, "Personal Values," p. 4, writes: "To increase its vitality, long life, and survival the family probably encourages self-orientation, family-orientation, and the development of individual power and influence by means of which the individual will be able to protect the self and the family. This last emphasis understandably leads to a great concern with personal power and the demonstration of its possession in a variety of ways." See also Wagley, *Latin American Tradition,* pp. 56–60; Adams, *Second Sowing,* pp. 158–60.

73. William J. Goode, "Industrialization and Family Change," in S. N. Eisenstadt, ed., *Comparative Perspectives on Social Change* (Boston: Little, Brown, 1968), pp. 47–52.

74. Chevalier, " 'Caudillos' et 'caciques' en Amérique," p. 44.

75. Ibid., p. 45.

76. On Cuban nepotism, see Irving L. Horowitz, "Cuban Communism," *Trans-Action* 4, no. 10 (October 1967): 86. Castro said, probably correctly, of the Batista government: "His regime brought merely a switch of hands and a redistribution of the loot among a new collection of friends, relatives, accomplices and parasitical dregs that constitute the political retinue of a dictator." Fidel Castro, *History Will Absolve Me* (London: Jonathan Cape, 1968), p. 86. On Perón's regime, see José Luis de Imaz, *Los que mandan* (Albany: State University Press of New York, 1970), pp. 15, 44–45; María Flores, "Another View of the Events of October," in Joseph R. Barager, ed., *Why Perón Came to Power* (New York: Knopf, 1968).

77. James A. Michener, *Iberia* (New York: Fawcett, 1969), p. 90. Something of the overlapping relationships of family and kin among French Canadians is suggested by Everett C. Hughes, *French Canada in Transition* (Chicago: University of Chicago Press, 1943), p. 164.

78. According to Chevalier, Trujillo "systematically agreed, and even used pressure to become the godfather of thousands of children, obviously in order to

create a tie of fidelity toward him with a large number of families, belonging by the way to all social classes including the most humble." " 'Caudillos' et 'caciques' en Amérique," p. 45.

79. Frank Brandenburg, "The Relevance of Mexican Experience to Latin American Development," in Norman A. Bailey, ed., *Latin America: Politics, Economics, and Hemispheric Security* (New York: Praeger, 1965), pp. 265–67.

80. John J. Johnson, *The Military and Society in Latin America* (Stanford: Stanford University Press, 1964), pp. 110–12. "In Cuba, dictator Fulgencio Batista was well aware that the Cuban armed forces were essential to his continuance in power, and he accordingly made great efforts to insure the loyalty of the forces. The Tabernilla family played a dominant role in his plans. The leader of this family was Major General Francisco J. Tabernilla y Dolz (with five stars, the only Cuban officer of the rank). A career army man, he was a second lieutenant when Batista staged the 'Sergeants' Revolt' in 1933. Tabernilla threw his lot in with Batista and subsequently became one of his closest friends. Promoted to lieutenant colonel in 1934, he made brigadier general in 1942. When Batista forces lost the election in 1944, Tabernilla was promptly 'retired.' Batista staged his last coup on March 10, 1952, with the active participation of Tabernilla, who was promoted to Major General and made Chief of Staff of the army. In January 1958, he was made Chief of the Joint General Staff and given the rank of General-in-Chief. He fled Cuba with Batista on January 1, 1959.

"General Tabernilla had three sons, Francisco, Carlos, and Marcelo. During 1957 and 1958, they held the following positions: Brigadier General Francisco H. Tabernilla y Palermo (two stars) was commanding officer of the Mixed Tank Regiment, which included all the tanks in the Cuban armed forces. Brigadier General Carlos M. Tabernilla y Palermo (one star) was commanding officer of the Cuban Army Air Force which, with the exception of a few antiquated navy planes, contained all the military aircraft Cuba had. Lieutenant Colonel Marcelo Tabernilla y Palermo, 'the baby of the family,' was commanding officer of the Cuban Army Air Force Bomber Squadron, which included all of the bombers Cuba possessed. In addition, the older Tabernilla's sister was married to Brigadier General Alberto Del Rio Chaviano (two stars), who spent most of the crucial years 1957 and 1958 as commanding officer of the Southern Military Zone of Oriente Province, which included the city of Santiago (Cuba's second largest) and the Sierra Maestra mountains, the center and heartland of Fidel Castro's operations."

81. Barzini, *The Italians*, p. 186. Madariaga points out that in Spanish life there are few who do not recognize the difference between formal learning and education in the customs and civilizing habits of a people. "Instinctively he knows that education and letters do not go more necessarily together than holiness and prayers." Salvador de Madariaga, *Spain* (New York: Creative Age Press, 1943), p. 69.

82. William J. McEwen, *Changing Rural Society: A Study of Communities in Bolivia* (London: Oxford University Press, 1975), p. 115.

83. See S. Walter Washington, "The Political Activity of Latin American Students," in Robert D. Tomasek, ed., *Latin American Politics* (Garden City, N.Y.: Anchor, 1966), pp. 115–27.

84. Note Wagley, *Latin American Tradition*, pp. 60–62.
85. For example, read Michener, *Iberia*, pp. 55–56.
86. Almond and Verba, *Civic Culture*, p. 304.
87. Caudillaje language typically allows for levels of address to distinguish levels of deference. See, e.g., Maraspini, *Italian Village*, pp. 141, 142; Rogelio Díaz-Guerrero, "Neurosis and the Mexican Family Structure," *American Journal of Psychiatry* 112, no. 6 (1955): 414.
88. For example, San Martín, liberator of the lower half of South America at the beginning of the nineteenth century, had a typical public-man beginning: "He organized the officers in a secret body." José Martí, *The America of José Martí*, trans. Juan de Onis (New York: Minerva Press, 1968), p. 180. Juan Manuel Rosas, the Argentine tyrant, did likewise: "The *Mazorca* which he founded was nothing else than a secret society." Cited in William Spence Robertson, "Foreign Estimates of the Argentine Dictator, Juan Manuel de Rosas," *Hispanic American Historical Review* 10 (1930): 135. Nearly a century and a quarter later another Argentine, Juan Perón, began in the same manner. On this tendency to form secret groups, see John J. Johnson, in Tomasek, *Latin American Politics*, pp. 106–7. It is important to note that these are not simply "pressure groups" in the accepted sense of the term. Rather, as Robert Potash points out in one of Johnson's footnotes, "more often than not the cliques are short-lived associations set up to advance the personal ambitions of certain officers" (p. 107).
89. Ernesto Landi, "Machiavelli," in Maurice Cranston, ed., *Western Political Philosophers* (New York: Capricorn Books, 1964), p. 42.
90. Italian Fascism jibed well with caudillaje values. War provided not a means of opening economic trade or redressing wrongs but rather a structure within which individual merit could be exhibited. As Mussolini declared, "War alone brings up to their highest tension all human energies and puts the stamp of nobility upon the people who have the courage to meet it.... War is to man what maternity is to the woman. I do not believe in perpetual peace; not only do I not believe in it, but I find it depressing and a negation of all the fundamental virtues of man." Cited by Levine, *Main Street Italy*, p. 71.
91. From Bonilla, *Failure of Elites*, p. 105.
92. It is true of course that historically speaking caudillaje society was founded upon personalistic criteria where "connections" were everything. See Eric Wolf, *Sons of the Shaking Earth* (Chicago: University of Chicago Press, 1962), p. 234.
93. Erich Fromm, *Man for Himself* (Greenwich, Conn.: Fawcett, 1969), p. 19. See also R. S. Peters, *Authority, Responsibility, and Education* (London: Allen & Unwin, 1959), pp. 40ff.; emphasis mine.
94. Freeman J. Wright, *Bureaucracy and Political Development: An Application of Almond and Powell to Latin America* (Tucson: University of Arizona, Institute of Government Research, 1970), p. 12, typifies the conventional wisdom on the relationship between bureaucracy and rationality. Planning is to be the panacea for Latin America as it brings with it rational procedures: "To the extent that a planner's outlook pervades day-to-day administration, bureaucratic decision-making grows closer to rational models."
95. Aldo E. Solari, *Estudios sobre la sociedad Uruguaya* (Montevideo: Arca,

1964), p. 162. English version can be found in Lipset and Solari, *Elites in Latin America*, p. 7. The same bias underlies the thinking of one of the more recent textbooks on Latin America. Edward J. Williams and Freeman J. Wright, *Latin American Politics* (Palo Alto: Mayfield, 1975), p. 431, write: "Friendships and political alliances are a more serious cause of particularistic hiring and promotion."

96. Jerry L. Weaver, "Value Patterns of a Latin American Bureaucracy" (Long Beach: California State College, 1969), p. 6. On friendship and bureaucratic procedures in Spain, see Díaz-Plaja, *El español*, pp. 264ff.

97. Maxwell, *Ten Pains of Death*, pp. 196–98.

98. René de Visme Williamson, *Culture and Policy: The United States and the Hispanic World* (Knoxville: University of Tennessee Press, 1949), p. 30.

99. Frank Bonilla, "The Urban Worker," in John J. Johnson, ed., *Continuity and Change in Latin America* (Stanford: Stanford University Press, 1964), p. 188. Bonilla sums up some remarks on urbanization by saying "these commonplace observations merit repetition here because of the persistent tendency to equate urban growth with economic expansion, industrialization, and other vaguely 'modernizing' forces. Yet in Latin America, the tide of urbanization (or at least the growth of urban agglomerations) seems to flow inexorably, irrespective of advances in the economy" (p. 186). Lambert, *Latin America*, p. 190, says flatly that in Latin America "urbanization proceeds independently of industrialization." On this general topic, see especially Alfred Stepan, "Political Development Theory: The Latin American Experience," *Journal of International Affairs* 20, no. 2 (1966): 223–34; Kingsley Davis and Ana Casis, "Urbanization in Latin America," in Olen E. Leonard and Charles P. Loomis, eds., *Readings in Latin American Social Organization and Istitutions* (East Lansing: Michigan State University Press, 1953), pp. 143–54; and Lars Schoultz, "Urbanization and Political Change in Latin America," *Midwest Journal of Political Science* 16, no. 3 (August 1972): 367–87.

Samuel J. Surace, *Ideology, Economic Change, and the Working Classes: The Case of Italy* (Berkeley: University of California Press, 1966), p. 72, after discussing rural-urban migration and its relationship to industrialization in Italy, notes "some interesting discrepancies in the data." For example, he points out, between the years 1901 and 1911 with a total in-migrant movement of 1.43 million persons, the total increase in persons employed in industry, transport, and commerce was only .77 million!

In Chile "the growth of the cities in every section of the country gives evidence that the rural worker and his family are no longer satisfied to remain in an environment that gives little hope for advancement or improvement." "This population growth, however, has not been accompanied by a proportional increment in industrialization." Cited in James Petras, *Politics and Social Structure in Latin America* (New York: Monthly Review Press, 1970), p. 76.

100. While I am convinced of this truth on an a priori basis, the only research I have found upon the matter is in Theodore Caplow, Sheldon Stryker, and Samuel E. Wallace, *Urban Ambience* (Totowa, N.J.: Bedminster Press, 1964), pp. 156–58. The authors compare United States and Puerto Rican degrees of "neighborliness."

101. Lewis, *Children of Sánchez*, p. 1.
102. Stepan, "Political Development," p. 231, writes that even though wages of the urban working class declined in a Brazilian study, nevertheless, "the *composition* of the class changed because of the constant addition of rural migrants who perceived a relative increase in environmental satisfaction." For a general statement on rural-urban migration in Latin America, see Smith, *Studies of Latin American Societies*, pp. 102–20, 339–71. Desbarats, *State of Quebec*, p. 5, has noticed that "with the exception of Ontario, Quebec today is the most 'urbanized' of all the Canadian provinces."

The desire to move to the cities appears to be particularly strong in Italy. In order to curb such movement in the 1930s the Fascist government restricted rural-urban migration by decree in 1931 and 1939. The latter, known as the antiurbanization law, stated that "no one may transfer his residence to capital cities of the kingdom's provinces, or to other localities with a population exceeding 25,000 inhabitants, or to cities of notable industrial importance, even if of smaller population, if he cannot show that he is compelled to make such a movement by his particular occupation, or if he has not previously found a profitable and stable occupation in the place of immigration, or if he has not been induced by other justifiable motives, and at all times only on the condition that the immigrant can show that he will not become a public charge in the place of immigration." Cited in Lopreato, *Peasants No More*, p. 31. Lopreato agrees with the position that emigration to the cities in Italy "is not primarily a question of seeking one's fortune" (p. 80). A suggestion as to how the law of internal emigration worked in practice can be seen in Ignazio Silone, *Fontamara* (New York: Harrison Smith & Robert Haas, 1934), pp. 81–82.
103. Magali Sarfatti, *Spanish Bureaucratic-Patrimonialism in America*, Politics of Modernization Series, no. 1 (Berkeley: University of California, 1966), p. 64.

CHAPTER II

1. Martin Luther, "The Freedom of a Christian," in John Dillenberger, ed., *Martin Luther: Selections from His Writings* (Garden City, N.Y.: Doubleday, 1961), p. 73. "In this life he must control his own body and have dealings with men. Here the works begin; here a man cannot enjoy leisure; here he must indeed take care to discipline his body" (p. 67).
2. *Poor Richard's Almanac* (Philadelphia: David McKay, n.d.), p. 14. The same world view underlay Thorstein Veblen's *The Theory of the Leisure Class* (New York: B. W. Huebsch, 1918). Leisure, he said, connotes "non-productive consumption of time" (p. 43).
3. Cited in Lipset, "Values, Education, and Entrepreneurship," p. 21.
4. Giuseppe di Lampedusa, *The Leopard*, trans. Archibald Colquhoun (New York: Pantheon, 1960), p. 246.
5. Pritchett, *Dublin*, p. 42.
6. Perceptive insights into the subject of time in these two cultures can be found in Edward T. Hall, *The Silent Language* (Greenwich, Conn.: Fawcett, 1959), p. 162.
7. Weber, *Protestant Ethic*, pp. 157–58.

8. Machiavelli, *Il principe*, p. 22.
9. Levine, *Main Street Italy*, p. 465. See also p. 45 for an Italian attitude toward time.
10. Brendan Behan, *Hold Your Hour and Have Another* (Boston: Little, Brown, 1954); see p. 21.
11. Lawrence L. Suhm, "Leisure in Latin America: A Preliminary Inquiry into the Economic and Social Implications of Mass Leisure in Underdeveloped Areas" (Ph.D. diss., University of Wisconsin, 1962), pp. 10, 1. George Brandes, *Poland: A Study of the Land, People, and Literature* (London: William Heinemann, 1903), p. 59. This view is supported by Barnett, *Poland*, pp. 405–6. Kurt Peter Karfield, *Austria in Color* (Vienna: Osterreichische Staatsdruckerei, 1957), p. 12. "Austria preaches and practices the philosophy of leisure," or *Gemütlichkeit*, says Karfield (ibid.).
12. Emilio Willems, "Culture Change and the Rise of Protestantism in Brazil and Chile," in S. N. Eisenstadt, ed., *The Protestant Ethic and Modernization* (New York: Basic Books, 1968), pp. 186–87.
13. Jorge Icaza, *Huasipungo* (Carbondale, Ill.: Southern Illinois University Press, 1964), p. 64.
14. Samuel Shapiro, *Invisible Latin America* (Boston: Beacon Press, 1963), pp. 8–9.
15. José Honorio Rodrígues, *The Brazilians: Their Character and Aspirations*, trans. Ralph E. Dimick (Austin: University of Texas Press, 1967), pp. 56–57.
16. "The people jeer at *pudientes* who, besides organizing, work with the *peones* on their land or personally take part in irrigation." Carmelo Lison-Tolosana, *Belmonte de los caballeros: A Sociological Study of a Spanish Town* (Oxford: Clarendon Press, 1966), p. 321. "For the most part the notables were admired for their ability to avoid a constant round of work." Barrett, *Benabarre*, p. 29.
17. Cornelisen, *Women of the Shadows*, p. 158.
18. Robert Theobald, *The Rich and the Poor* (New York: C. N. Potter, 1960), p. 31.
19. José Enrique Rodó, *Ariel* (Buenos Aires: Kapelusz, 1966), p. 39.
20. Domingo Arena, *Batlle y los problemas sociales en el Uruguay* (Montevideo, n.d.), pp. 109–10.
21. There is an old Haitian proverb that "if work were a good thing, the rich would have grabbed it all long ago." Selden Rodman, *Haiti: The Black Republic* (New York: Devin-Adair, 1954), p. 34. While I don't know anything about the spirit of caudillaje in Haiti, it is easy to foresee that with proverbs like this Marxism finds natural support.
22. Here an intentional parallel has been drawn with Weber's observations on Ben Franklin's moral attitudes. See *Protestant Ethic*, p. 52.
23. Levine, *Main Street Italy*, p. 21.
24. "The Social Class Structure," *Materiales para el estudio de la clase media en la America Latina* (Washington, D.C.: Pan American Union, 1950), 2: 54.
25. From a conversation recorded in Ronald Fraser, *The Pueblo: A Mountain Village on the Costa del Sol* (London: Allen Lane, 1973), p. 205.
26. From Johnson, *Continuity and Change*, pp. 76–77. In the pueblo of Aritama, "for those children who attend school, the methods employed in teaching

have a far-reaching influence. In the first place, the child is systematically taught the high prestige value of good clothes and of ceremonial behavior, and is made to abhor and to ridicule all manual labor and cooperative effort.... They are taught that 'work' (*trabajo*) is to be avoided, but that 'employment' (*empleo*) is to be sought, as a sinecure well deserved by anyone who has attended school." Gerardo and Alicia Reichel-Dolmatoff, *The People of Aritama: The Cultural Personality of a Colombian Mestizo Village* (Chicago: University of Chicago Press, 1961), pp. 124–25. See also Wagley, *Latin American Tradition*, p. 53. Menéndez Pidal, *Spaniards in Their History*, p. 21, sums up the impressions of a traveler to historical Spain: "He did not describe the Andalusian workman as lazy, but noted that as soon as he had gathered a handful of reals, he would throw his embroidered jacket over his shoulder, pick up his guitar and go off to sport among his friends or pay court to the girls, until lack of money would force him to return to work. This interruption of work was not a daily occurrence and was not caused by exhaustion necessitating long periods of rest for rebuilding energy, but by a weakening of the stimulus to work. Once his urgent material necessities had been satisfied, his attention would wander off after other incentives which appeared more attractive." Modern Spain, apparently, has not changed this attitude toward work. "By working one seeks to achieve the ideal of life, which is 'to live without working,'" says Lison-Tolosana of the Spanish in *Belmonte de los caballeros*, p. 321. According to Díaz-Plaja, *El español*, p. 253, "el origen del trabajo es la maldición bíblica. Esta verdad nunca ha sido tan clara como en España, donde el individuo, por humilde que sea su nacimiento, por pobre que sea el ambiente en que ha crecido, no considera el trabajo lógica consecuencia de su existencia, sino como una condena, que el tiene que cumplir sin culpa alguna."

27. From Barzini, *The Italians*, pp. 118–19.
28. *Il principe*, p. 64.
29. Of Ireland, he says. "We have an aristocracy of personality! There is a kind of classlessness in Irish society because we are interested in a man's mind and personality instead of his title or income. A commoner will be more readily accepted than a prince if he is a more interesting person." Cited by Connery, *The Irish*, p. 91. Pritchett, *Dublin*, p. 44, speaks of "the cult of personality."
30. J. Alexander Mahan, *Vienna of Yesterday and Today* (Vienna: The Vienna Times, 1928), p. 234.
31. Machado de Assis, *The Psychiatrist and Other Stories*, trans. William L. Grossman and Helen Caldwell (Berkeley: University of California Press, 1966), p. 118.
32. Cited by Robertson, "Foreign Estimates," p. 134.
33. Barzini, *The Italians*, p. 141.
34. R. H. Phillips, *Cuba, Island of Paradox* (New York: McDowell, Obolensky, 1959), p. 293. Herbert Matthews says that Castro "is certainly one of the most brilliant talkers I have ever met." *Fidel Castro* (New York: Simon & Schuster, 1969), p. 30.
35. Mariano Azuela, *Los de abajo*, chap. 10. A similar moral is drawn in Ricardo Güiraldes, *Don segundo sombra* (New York: Signet, 1966), a novel of the usually silent gaucho. The hero is an accomplished tale spinner, a talent

which "added luster to his fame" (p. 69), and also able at the tradition of making up spontaneous verses to music that fit the occasion (pp. 78–79).

36. *Iberia*, p. 73. Díaz-Plaja, *El español*, p. 58, adds that "el silencio, para nosotros, equivale a la abolicion."

37. Cited by Joe McCarthy, *Ireland* (New York: Time, 1964), p. 29. For an example of the content of a classic Irish pubside oration, see *Charles Lever*, "Billy Traynor as Orator," in John McCarthy, *The Home Book of Irish Humor*, pp. 127–33; for an example of a Latin American pubside oration, see Asturias, *El señor presidente*, pp. 255–56.

38. Edwin Cerio, *That Capri Air* (London: William Heinemann, 1929), p. 3.

39. Lewis, *Children of Sánchez*, p. 431. Typically, the great Italian revolutionary of the nineteenth century, Garibaldi, was adept at declaiming poetry, both his own and that of others. See Denis M. Smith, ed., *Garibaldi* (Englewood Cliffs, N.J.: Prentice-Hall, 1969), p. 93.

40. From Maxwell, *Ten Pains of Death*, p. 138.

41. Journalism is held in very high esteem in Catholic culture for this same reason. It is a perceivable public excellence. Thus Mussolini was not only an accomplished public speaker but "perhaps the best popular journalist of his day in Italy." Barzini, *The Italians*, p. 142. A journalist in caudillaje culture usually goes well beyond the facts. Unlike capitalist man, he focuses upon "truth" rather than "fact." Perhaps this is because journalists' and orators' first ambitions were toward poetry and philosophy. G. A. Borgese wrote, "often, a poet who has failed becomes a journalist, a philosopher who has failed becomes an orator. This happened to Mussolini too. He is renowned the world over as a great journalist and orator." From A. William Salomone, ed., *Italy from the Risorgimento to Fascism* (New York: Anchor, 1970), p. 168.

42. Walter Bryan, *The Improbable Irish* (New York: Taplinger, 1969), p. 148.

43. Marie Henri Beyle [Stendhal], *Shorter Novels of Stendhal*, trans. C. K. Scott-Moncrieff (New York: Liveright, 1946), p. 12.

44. My thesis is that this world view dominates *all* of caudillaje culture today. One can appreciate the truth of that observation, for example, by looking to the lower class in southern Italy. There, it is reported, "everyone tries to distinguish himself, which explains the importance that certain formal facts assume: to dress with affectation becomes a symbol of social position, whereby, in the words of an interviewee, 'many prefer not to eat but to spend almost all that they have in clothing.' The display of jewelry and gold objects, on the part of men as well as women, has the same emulative meaning, while, despite aspirations declared by almost all, little is spent for the home, where few ever enter." Lopreato, *Peasants No More*, pp. 73–74.

45. Cited by Levine, *Main Street Italy*, p. 350.

46. Thomas R. Fillol, *Social Factors in Economic Development: The Argentine Case* (Cambridge: MIT Press, 1961), p. 18, says that when an Argentine wants to advance, "he will usually try to do so, not by developing his manual skills or by accomplishing business or industrial feats, but by developing his *intellectual* skills. He will follow an academic point of view—medicine, law, social sciences, etc." See also Lipset, "Values, Education, and Entrepreneurship," p. 20. In the past ten years sociology has come into its own in Latin America. There is little question that this occurred due to the affinity between

public-man values and perceived opportunities for social (public) engineering through sociological expertise. In Chile, for example, the relationship between sociology and planning has been close. Elites holding that orientation were enormously influential in both the Christian Democratic party of Frei and the Marxist party of Allende. Carmen Barros, "Sociology in Chile" (Paper presented at Pacific Coast Conference on Latin American Studies, University of California at Santa Barbara, November 1970). In short, "the whole public education system [of Latin America] has been organized as a preparation for higher education, and more particularly for the type of education provided in the faculties of law, which gave instruction not only in law but also in political and social science, for a class of leaders." Jacques Lambert, "Requirements for Rapid Economic and Social Development," in Egbert de Vries and José Medina Echavarria, eds., *Social Aspects of Economic Development in Latin America* (Paris: UNESCO, 1963), 1: 64.

47. Cited in Lipset, "Values, Education, and Entrepreneurship," p. 22.

48. Maxwell, *Ten Pains of Death*, p. 240. In Poland, "to confess that one was wrong is a matter of great shame and Poles find it hard to understand a person who has honestly changed his mind." Barnett, *Poland*, p. 399.

49. Maxwell, *Ten Pains of Death*, p. 184.

50. Aristotle, *Politics*, bks. 7 and 8; *Ethics*. Machiavelli in his *Discorsi*, bk. 1. chap. 18, stressed the need for good habits. Bolívar despaired of the "bad" habits engrained in Latin Americans over the centuries. See *Selected Writings of Bolívar*, p. 75. Spanish despotism had warped the psychology of man in the New World, thought Bolívar. He saw the difficulty in uplifting and changing these habits of mind: "Our hands are now free, but our hearts still suffer the ills of slavery. When man loses freedom, said Homer, he loses half his spirit" (p. 183). Bolívar credited the Spaniards with teaching well only one habit, that of obedience (p. 105).

51. Asturias, *El señor presidente*, p. 32.

52. *Selected Writings of Bolívar*, p. 558. Bolívar goes on: "This is not a trifling matter. It is of such practical importance that its neglect gives rise to quarrels, enmity, and grief." In a letter to his nephew, Bolívar wrote: "Instruction in good breeding and social behavior is as essential as formal teaching; for this reason special care should be taken that he learn the code and manners of a gentleman from Lord Chesterfield's letters to his son" (p. 310).

53. Wagley, *Latin American Tradition*, p. 54.

54. Pitts, "Change in Bourgeois France," p. 242.

55. Ibid., p. 243.

56. Lison-Tolosana, *Belmonte de los caballeros*, p. 324.

57. Morris West, for example, gives away his Protestant ethical background while recording observations on Naples: "They are a Catholic people, as I am a Catholic, yet their social ethics are as pagan as those of Pompeii and the Rome of Tiberius." Morris L. West, *Children of the Shadows* (New York: William Morrow, 1957), p. 46.

58. "The Social Class Structure," in Robert F. Smith, ed., *Background to Revolution: The Development of Modern Cuba* (New York: Knopf, 1966), p. 199.

59. On charity among French Canadians, see Desbarats, *State of Quebec*, pp. 33ff. According to Desbarats, the French Canadian "idea of the individual citizen's

role in a democratic society leaves relatively little room for private action and responsibility" (p. 34).

60. "La existencia del mendigo, alguien a quien dar, es esencial para la seguridad interna del español," writes Díaz-Plaja, *El español*, p. 20.

61. From *Pro Sestio oratio*, reprinted in Ernest Barker, *From Alexander to Constantine* (London: Oxford University Press, 1956), p. 203.

62. Carlos Fuentes, *The Death of Artemio Cruz* (New York: Noonday, 1964), p. 113.

63. Another contraposition is that between dignity and liberty. María Flores says that for a *porteño* "a loss of dignity can be more important than a loss of liberty." Cited in Barager, *Why Perón Came to Power*, p. 207. See also p. 213.

64. These values can be seen as operative upon the international level also. For example, the United States initiated the program "Operation Intercept" on the Mexican border in 1969 to cut down on the smuggling of marijuana. The Mexicans responded with a counterplan called "Operation Dignity" which "kept tens of thousands of Mexicans from visiting the United States during the ill-fated three weeks." Latin American Digest 4, no. 2 (November 1969): 1.

65. I believe Melvin Tumin and Arnold Feldman are only partially correct when they point to a Puerto Rican "belief that all men are ultimately equal and equally worthy of respect, regardless of temporary or even enduring differences in their material standard of living, in the formal power they exercise, or in the prestige which their occupations and educations evoke." *Social Class and Social Change in Puerto Rico* (Princeton: Princeton University Press, 1961), p. 18. What seems more valid is to say that Puerto Ricans whatever their status attempt at least a certain equalitarian *dignidad* among their peer group.

66. La Souchère, *Explanation of Spain*, p. 29. See also Díaz-Plaja, *El español*, pp. 89–90.

67. Barnett, *Poland*, pp. 398–99. At least some caudillaje languages permit one to avoid fixing responsibility for personal fallibilities and thus maintain another's integrity intact. For example, in Spanish, if someone drops his coffee cup, it is possible for the host to call a maid explaining that "the cup fell" or that "it broke itself."

68. For example, see John A. Mackay, *The Other Spanish Christ: A Study in the Spiritual History of Spain and South America* (New York: Macmillan, 1932), chap. 1; and Gillin, "Ethos Components," pp. 507–8. Américo Castro says, "let us not go on calling this rebellious and proud aloofness 'individualism.' It would be better to approach this strange and sometimes splendid kind of existence as a 'personal absolutism.' " *The Structure of Spanish History* (Princeton: Princeton University Press, 1954), p. 623. He might have added that the utility of this personal absolutism has been found in its aggregation function.

69. The word *credit* in capitalistic societies has the ring of contracts fulfilled in the past albeit usually between strangers. In caudillaje culture, financial credit follows social credit—it is usually very personal and based upon rational calculation. In general, then, "credit is not extended, for it is assumed that the risk is too great if lending occurs outside the web of face-to-face relations, where the fulfillment of financial obligations can be supported by informal social sanctions." Díaz, *Tonalá*, p. 205.

70. Lewis, *Children of Sánchez*, p. 38.

71. Consuelo, in ibid., p. 126. Also see Oscar Lewis, *Tepoztlán* (New York: Henry Holt, 1960), pp. 86ff.

72. Silone, *Fontamara*, p. 227.

73. Lison-Tolosana, *Belmonte de los caballeros*, p. 326. "All groups share alike this drive towards rivalry in some form or other; they are all subject to this one inner demand, this one *vigencia:* to prove through concrete manifestations their manliness, their personal worth" (p. 324).

74. Pitt-Rivers, *People of the Sierra*, p. 157.

75. Thomas G. Sanders, "The Social Functions of Futebol," *American Universities Field Staff Reports* (East Coast South America Series), 14, no. 2: 2. On the importance of soccer in Latin America, see Ernest Hecht, "Football," in Claudio Véliz, ed., *Latin America and the Caribbean* (New York: Praeger, 1968), pp. 743–48.

76. Hughes, *French Canada in Transition*, p. 166.

77. Williamson, *Culture and Policy*, p. 36.

78. Williamson says: "It is no question of money, prestige, or position. Those things are present but they are completely overshadowed by the central fact that what is at stake is life itself: the life of the horses, the bulls, and the bullfighters" (ibid.).

79. "The bullfighter symbolizes the Cid Campeador who fought to drive out the infidels, the inquisitor who fought to clear the country of heretics, the *Conquistador* who set out to subjugate a continent, Ignatius Loyola who organized the Company of Jesus and trained its members with spiritual exercises for a spiritual combat to reconquer the obviously tangible territories of Protestant Europe" (ibid., p. 37).

80. *America of José Martí*, p. 169. Elsewhere in the essay Martí refers to "the manliness of his [Páez's] conduct."

81. William MacCann, *Two Thousand Miles' Ride through the Argentine Provinces* (London: Smith, Elder, 1853), 2: 4. William Spence Robertson refers to a French observer of carnival in Buenos Aires who said: "No one can tame a colt, or break a savage horse, or hunt a cougar better than Rosas. He made a show of compelling his fine Chilean steed to gallop through the worst paved streets of the capital; then he would suddenly wheel about, retrace his steps, and pirouette over the slippery stones, dodging not only the buckets of water but also the eggs which on that day, according to custom, the women showered upon the passerby." "Foreign Estimates," p. 127. Another partisan of Rosas wrote in the *Gaceta mercantil* of Buenos Aires: "The dexterity, agility, and hardihood of General Rosas in horsemanship and in exercises of strength, are perhaps unequalled in the Republic, as well as his ability, experience, and knowledge with respect to all sorts of rural labors and customs. But I should add that to these estimable gifts he unites other eminent qualities; his talents, his vast knowledge, his political skill and judgment, and his valor in military campaigns have often saved the republic from ruin and desolation. Classic and luminous proofs of this truth are furnished by his public life from the memorable year 1820 until the present time. He is the only man among us who has known how to unite the administrative talents of a most consummate statesman with the intrepidity, agility, and bravery of a warrior, and with

traits of a most clever gaucho. Then we must add to this happy union of singular and necessary qualities, an unshakeable patriotism, a severe virtue, and a noble disinterestedness—a combination of qualities that makes him the most perfect exemplar of the politician, the hero, the warrior, and the great citizen" (ibid.).

82. João Guimarães Rosa, *The Devil to Pay in the Backlands* (New York: Knopf, 1963), p. 109.

83. Octavio Paz, *The Labyrinth of Solitude* (New York: Grove Press, 1961), p. 79.

84. Guevara, *Venceremos!*, p. 132.

85. Adams, "Political Power and Social Structure," pp. 24–25.

86. *Tonalá*, p. 108. In his *Second Sowing*, Adams specifically divides the value systems of the upper and lower sectors—conceding that power pertains to the upper sector while allocating materialism and work to the lower sector! "The two sectors have both distinctive value systems and different bases for social mobility. They do, however, manifest some parallel structural features. The lower sector has wealth as its goal, and the recognized means to obtain it is work. The upper sector has a variety of prestige symbols as its goal, and the means of achieving them lie in the manipulation of power" (p. 48). See also p. 257. Adams does agree, however, that power in Latin America is somehow more extensive than in other areas. "This 'concern for power' should be distinguished from the hard power realities of government. The latter are found in all governments and in no sense can be said to be uniquely Latin. The bases of power upon which a government rests, the manipulations necessary, the balancing of interests and controls, and so on, are all to be found in politics and administration anywhere. The 'concern for power,' however, is specifically important in Latin American governments; the manipulation of power by politicians is given a value quite beyond its utilitarian foundations and indeed may be said to be a matter that is raised to something of an art among its practitioners" (pp. 179–80). And, he notes elsewhere, "I do not think that the major features of this kind of power structures are necessarily transitional phenomena, nor must we anticipate that Latin American society will eventually shift over to a structure more like that of Anglo-American culture" (p. 59).

87. *The Autobiography of Benjamin Franklin* (New York: Modern Library, 1944), p. 75.

88. Goodman, *Benjamin Franklin Reader*, p. 128.

89. Weber, *Protestant Ethic*, p. 52.

90. John Calvin, *Institutes of the Christian Religion* (1636), bk 3, chap. 19, par. 2.

91. Adam Smith, "Theory of Moral Sentiments," in Schneider, ed., *Adam Smith's Moral and Political Philosophy*, p. 231.

92. Machiavelli, *Il principe*, p. 73.

93. Machiavelli, *Discorsi*, p. 192.

94. Quoted by Cornelisen, *Torregreca*, p. 105.

95. Barzini, *The Italians*, p. 88. "In normal times, after all, when there are no conflicts, power and the show of power can be considered equivalent" (p. 87). Public men in caudillaje culture lose no opportunity to have their prominent attributes recorded for posterity. The heights of such publications are suggested by Bonilla, *Failure of Elites*, p. 53.

96. Díaz-Plaja, *El español*, p. 30.
97. Cited by Robertson, "Foreign Estimates," p. 134.
98. Díaz-Plaja, *El español*, p. 91, feels that "appearance is sacred in Spain."
99. Maxwell, *Ten Pains of Death*, p. 44. In Bolivia it is difficult to negotiate a bank loan. "Some rules eliminate potential borrowers for no relevant reasons. For example, there is a rule that bank engineers who appraise property must travel by jeep. But many loan-worthy properties cannot be reached by jeep. No jeep, no appraisers; no appraisers, no loans." McEwen, *Changing Rural Society*, p. 34.
100. Although one sees some machismo attributes on beaches of Protestant-ethic cultures, such activity does not predominate because when accompanied by several partners the esteem rewards probably seem too limited. While Catholic-ethic peoples almost never sunbathe, such passive behavior is embraced by Protestant-ethic peoples because it can be seen as a significant activity. One can return home showing that one *accomplished* something, i.e., one got a suntan. Time was not wasted.
101. Erik H. Erikson, *Insight and Responsibility* (New York: Norton, 1964), p. 113, expands upon this information.
102. Marcus Tullius Cicero, *On Duties*, trans. Herbert M. Poteat (Chicago: University of Chicago Press, 1950), p. 499.
103. Karl Vossler, *Algunas carácteres de la cultura española*, 4th ed. (Madrid: Espasa-Calpe, 1962), p. 13.
104. Mead in studying Spanish Americans of New Mexico found that machismo is not related to work. "Their feeling of masculine purpose and dignity does not depend on holding a job." Margaret Mead, ed., *Cultural Patterns and Technical Change* (New York, 1955), pp. 164–65.
105. Gillin, "Ethos Components," p. 509.
106. Nelson, *Waiting Village*, p. 75.
107. Leo T. Mahon, "Machismo and Christianity," *Catholic Mind* 63, no. 1190 (February 1965): 4–11.
108. Nelson, *Waiting Village*, p. 74. According to this author, "the villagers look upon Joseph as a sort of fool. There are jokes that refer to him as an impotent, very unmasculine man *(un pendejo)*" (p. 68).
109. La Souchère, *Explanation of Spain*, p. 14.
110. Díaz-Plaja, *El español*, p. 43.
111. Ibid., p. 132.
112. The conquistador psychology of mestizos has been outlined by Santiago Ramírez, *El mexicano, psicología de sus motivaciones* (Mexico: Editorial Pax-Mexico, 1961), pp. 64–65. Fidel Castro in a famous speech defending his actions at the Moncada Barracks said of the torture of his fellow revolutionaries: "Even when they had been deprived of their virile organs, our men were still a thousand times more manly than all their tormentors together." *History Will Absolve Me*, p. 65. During a dispute at a Sicilian *festa*, one of the principals boasts: "Attentu comu ti metti viri ca li mei cugghiuna sunnu chiu grossi di li toi." Maxwell, *Ten Pains of Death*, p. 266. Also see p. 152.
113. Santos, "Personal Values," p. 4.
114. Ignazio Silone portrays the Italian peasant's incredulity in the face of man-initiated change in the flow of a stream of water: "It would mean the end

of everything if man's will should get to extending its power over the elements created by God, if it should start out changing the direction of the winds, the track of the sun, the course of water, all of them fixed by God Almighty. It would be like somebody claiming donkeys were going to take up flying or that Prince Torlonia was about to quit being a prince, or that farmers were going to stop suffering from hunger; in a word, as though the laws of God were going to stop being the laws of God." *Fontamara*, p. 29.

115. Barnett, *Poland*, p. 352.

116. José María Argüedas, *Yawar Fiesta* (Lima: Populibros peruanos, n.d.), p. 12.

117. Ciro Alegría, *Broad and Alien Is the World* (Toronto: Farrar & Rinehart, 1941), p. 165.

118. William V. D'Antonio and Frederick B. Pike, *Religion, Revolution, and Reform* (New York: Praeger, 1964), p. 126.

119. Stanislav Andreski, *Parasitism and Subversion: The Case of Latin America* (New York: Schocken, 1969), p. 43.

120. Samuel Ramos gives us a cryptic, if unintentional, summary of the two ethics by contrasting the products of the European with the Mexican. Mexicans look at the world and say, "A European has science, art, technical knowledge, and so forth; we have none of that here, but...we are very manly." Ramos continues, "manly in the zoological sense of the term, that is, in the sense of the male enjoying complete animal potency." *Profile of Man and Culture in Mexico*, trans. Peter Earle (New York: McGraw-Hill, 1962), p. 61. Mexico appears to be the caudillaje society most prone to make references to the physiological side of machismo. See, for example, Fuentes, *Death of Artemio Cruz*, pp. 113-14; Lewis, *Children of Sánchez*, pp. 440-41, 431, 38; Díaz-Guerrero, "Neurosis and the Mexican Family Structure," pp. 411-17; Salvador Reyes Nevares, "El machismo en Mexico," *Mundo nuevo*, April 1970, pp. 14-19.

Machismo is undoubtedly as prominent in Latin America today as it was three centuries ago. The guerrilla bands seem to have accentuated this virtue. Irving Horowitz maintains that "the guerrilla is the incarnation of *machismo*." "In Cuba," he says, "the elevation of proletarian *machismo* has become official policy." "Cuban Communism," p. 9.

121. Paz, *Labyrinth of Solitude*, p. 82. "One word sums up the aggressiveness, insensitivity, invulnerability and other attributes of the macho: power" (p. 81). Roberto Sánchez suggests that the "law of the strongest operates here." Lewis, *Children of Sánchez*, p. 232. Consuelo Sánchez says that the "law of the strongest" does not belong only to the male: "There is no way except to follow the wishes of the strongest ones. After my father, Antonia had her way, then La Chata, then my brothers. The weaker ones could approve or disapprove, get angry or disgusted but could never express their opinions" (p. 237). The dysfunctional nature of capitalistic qualifications as a means to advancement within caudillaje culture is outlined by the Bolivian, Alcides Argüedas: "Las aptitudes, la especialización, el technicismo no cuentan. Tampoco la experiencia ni la honestidad; pero juegan rol preponderante en la elección de los nuevos empleados de toda categoría, tanto del interior como diplomáticos y consulares, el parentesco, la amistad, el servicio recibido, cuando no el deseo de quebrantar una oposición, reducir y acallar a un ad-

versario.... Y el país, naturalmente, retrocede, se empobrece y debilita porque las 'gloriosas' sólo significan, en la mayoría de los casos, la ascensión al poder de gentes mediocres, sin preparación técnica ni profesional, pero llenas de apetitos groseros, ya que sólo en el cambio de posición y de fortuna alcanzan a ver la manera más fácil de amasar fortuna y enriquecer, entrando en combinaciones oscuras y maniobrando sin pudor y con desplante, pero con la complicidad regocijada o interesada del superior." Alcides Argüedas, *Pueblo enfermo* (Santiago, Chile: Ediciones Ercilla, 1937), p. 222.

Samuel Ramos seeks to characterize the relationship between sexual virility and power which pervades the outlook of some Mexicans. "The most destitute of Mexican *pelados* consoles himself by shouting at everyone that 'he's got balls' (*muchos huevos*) with reference to the testicles. It is important to note that he attributes to the reproductive organ not only one kind of potency, the sexual, but every kind of human power. In the *pelado* a man who triumphs in any activity, anywhere, owes his success to his 'balls.' Another of his favorite expressions, 'I am your father' (*Yo soy tu padre*), intends to assert his predominance unequivocally. In our patriarchal societies the father is for all men the symbol of power. It must also be remarked that the *pelado*'s phallic obsession is not comparable to phallic cults and their underlying notions of fecundity and eternal life. The phallus suggests to the *pelado* the idea of power. From this he has derived a very impoverished concept of man. Since he is, in effect, a being without substance, he tries to fill his void with the only suggestive force accessible to him: that of the male animal." *Man and Culture in Mexico*, pp. 60–61.

122. François Bourricaud, *Power and Society in Contemporary Peru* (London: Faber & Faber, 1970), pp. 36–37, writes, "But what is the real significance of the social and physical power which they [the *patrones*] enjoy—a power which might almost be called 'virile,' in view of the sexual connotation of the word *macho* (male) which the rulers of this society like to hear used of themselves."

123. Juan de Onis, "The Opposition in Chile," *New York Times Magazine*, December 17, 1972, p. 84. According to Manuel, "Mexicans, and I think everyone in the world, admire the person 'with balls,' as we say. The character who throws punches and kicks, without stopping to think, is the one who comes out on top. The one who has guts enough to stand up against an older, stronger guy, is more respected.... In a fight, I would never give up or say, 'Enough,' even though the other was killing me. I would try to go to my death, smiling. That is what we mean by being '*macho*,' by being manly." Lewis, *Children of Sánchez*, p. 38.

124. Díaz-Plaja, *El español*, p. 20.

125. In an Italian village a little boy "never hears himself referred to otherwise but as '*il maschietto*.'... So that, by the time he has reached maturity, he has been conditioned to regard virility as equivalent to manliness." Maraspini, *Italian Village*, p. 152.

126. Julio Mafud, *Psicología de la viveza criolla* (Buenos Aires: Editorial Americalee, 1971), p. 61. "Hay un término en el vocabulario masculino que expresa maravillosamente el estado del sujeto que dice abiertamente que esta enamo-

rado: es un 'reblandecido.' Obsérvese el significado del vocablo en oposición a 'endurecido,' que esta en absoluto vinculado a la virilidad" (ibid.).

127. *La prensa* (Managua, Nicaragua), March 25, 1974, p. 6.

128. Edith Hamilton, *The Roman Way* (New York: Mentor, 1957), p. 128.

129. Livy, *History of Rome*, bk. 39, p. 40.

130. Ibid., bk. 21, p. 4.

131. Suetonius, *The Lives of the Twelve Caesars* (New York: Modern Library, 1931), p. 34.

132. Machiavelli, "The Life of Castruccio Castracani of Lucca," *Machiavelli: The Chief Works and Others*, trans. Allan Gilbert (Durham, N.C.: Duke University Press, 1965), 2: 536. "In Castruccio charm increased with the years, and in everything he showed ability and prudence, and quickly, according to his age, he learned the things to which he was directed by Messer Antonio, who, intending to make him a priest and in time to turn over to his canonry and other benefices, according to that purpose taught him. But he had found a subject wholly alien to the priestly character, for as soon as Castruccio reached the age of fourteen began to get a little courage in respect to Messer Antonio and not to fear Madonna Dianora at all, laying churchly books aside, he began to busy himself with weapons; he took delight in nothing else than in handling or, with his companions, in running, jumping, wrestling and similar sports, in which he showed the utmost strength and far surpassed all others of his age. If he did at any time, no other reading pleased him than that which dealt with war or with things done by the greatest men. On account of this, Messer Antonio suffered immeasurable unhappiness and distress" (p. 535).

133. Matteo Palmieri, *Della vita civile* (Milan: G. Silvestri, 1825), p. 136.

134. Fuentes, *Death of Artemio Cruz*, p. 117.

135. Nelson, *Waiting Village*, p. 108.

136. Ibid., p. 116.

137. Ibid., p. 117.

138. Fuentes, *Death of Artemio Cruz*, p. 259. The same theme dominates German E. Ornes, *Trujillo: Little Caesar of the Caribbean* (New York: Thomas Nelson, 1958). In his preface Ornes argues that Trujillo was engaged in one clear goal: "the search for and safekeeping of power for power's sake." Gaudens Megaro early sketched this direction in Mussolini's life. He writes, "the one concern from which he has never swerved has been his search for power." Megaro then predicted: "And yet, great as his victory in Ethiopia has been, it has by no means appeased his thirst for personal glory. As long as Mussolini lives as the head of the Italian State, the world will know no peace, for this man's constant and restless search for power knows no bounds and no restraint." Salomone, *Italy from the Risorgimento*, pp. 259–60.

139. Machiavelli, *Discorsi*, p. 163.

140. Salvador de Madariaga, *Spain: A Modern History* (New York: Praeger, 1958), p. 23.

141. Maxwell, *Ten Pains of Death*, p. 197.

142. "Ethos Components," p. 509.

143. Ramírez, *El mexicano*, p. 63. See also Wolfgang A. Luchting, "Machismus moribundus?" *Mundo nuevo*, no. 23 (May 1968), pp. 61–67.

144. Martí, *America of José Martí*, p. 203.

145. Giuseppe Tomasi di Lampedusa in his novel of the Italian risorgimento, *Il gattopardo*, writes knowingly upon the subject of power and the new man. The Prince, head of an old established family, is made to advance the candidacy of such a person. "There is a name I should like to suggest for the Senate: that of Calogero Sedàra. He has more the qualities to sit there than I have: his family, I am told, is an old one or soon will be; he has more than what you call prestige, he has power; he has outstanding practical merits instead of scientific ones; his attitude during the May crisis was not so much irreproachable as actively useful; as to illusions, I don't think he has any more than I have, but he's clever enough to know how to create them when needed. He's the man for you. But you must be quick, as I've heard that he intends to put up as candidate for the Chamber of Deputies." *Il gattopardo* (Milano: Feltrinelli Editore, 1959), p. 214.

146. Figures cited by Almond and Verba, *Civic Culture*, chap. 6, bear out this fact. In general, however, their conclusions on political participation, partisanship, etc., should not be taken at face value. The authors have collected their data within the framework of capitalistic values, forgetting that caudillaje man takes his bearings from immediate power possibilities rather than from the formal political arrangements of the nation. Hence, for example, while Italians and Mexicans talk interminably about power in the immediate sense of influencing people, according to Almond and Verba their "frequency of talking politics with other people" is very low (p. 116). Caudillaje man cannot understand questionnaires and "public" opinion polls. After all, what he says and his "opinion" depend upon his public. He sees nothing unusual or unethical about this. As a matter of fact, to charge him with a lack of ethics is to misunderstand his whole world view. Thus, social-science research on Latin America, to the extent that it relies upon survey data, is bound to be less than satisfactory. Imagine Machiavelli, the public man, giving an "honest" answer to a political questionnaire! It is absurd to even ask him to respond. In terms of his code of ethics, the situation—even, we may assume, the situation of being interviewed—determines one's response.

147. In this I take exception to the usual social scientism which claims to see dysfunction in such personalistic activity. A recent exponent of this view is Evelyn P. Stevens, "Mexican Machismo: Politics and Value Orientations," in Paul Kramer and Robert E. McNicoll, eds., *Latin American Panorama* (New York: Capricorn, 1968), pp. 401–2: "Today, as in the past, no self-respecting Mexican would admit to being anything but a *macho completo* (100 percent male). But because of decisions politically made and politically implemented, he is free to conduct certain crucial activities according to *other, more rational criteria*" (emphasis mine).

148. Émile Durkheim, *Suicide* (New York: Free Press, 1951), p. 353. Note Maurice L. Farber, "Psychocultural Variables in Italian Suicide," in Norman L. Farberow, *Suicide in Different Cultures* (Baltimore: University Park Press, 1975), pp. 179–84. See also María Luisa Rodríguez-Sola de Gomezgil, *Suicidios y*

suicidas en la sociedadas mexicana (Mexico: Instituto de Investigaciones Sociales, 1974), p. 12.

149. María Elvira Bermúdez, *La vida familiar del mexicano* (Mexico: Antigua Librería Robredo, 1955), pp. 88–90, points out that in Mexico "un macho no puede ser vencido" and that Mexico occupies second place in the world in number of homicides.

150. An anthropologist, Cynthia Nelson, showed a picture of a "woman with hands around throat of a second woman" to Mexican villagers and asked them to make up a story about the picture. Nelson concludes: "Significant in this story is the lack of guilt over an aggressive and violent act. This is indicative of Erongaricuarenos in general. Villagers direct their aggression and hostility outward rather than inward against the self—which may account for the relatively few stories about suicide.... Based upon this analysis what bothers most Erongaricuarenos is the transgression against authority, particularly parental authority. However, the guilt engendered by such transgression does not become internalized as a motive for achievement as it does in other cultures." *Waiting Village*, p. 120.

151. Tad Szulc, *Twilight of the Tyrants* (New York: Henry Holt, 1959), p. 97.

CHAPTER III

1. Barzini, *The Italians*, p. 202. Nicholas Pileggi, writing about Frank Mari, the Cosa Nostra leader, points to the extreme public-private dichotomy of participants in this archetypal Catholic organization: "Like most mafiosi, Mari did not associate with anyone who was not either a member or related to a member of that exotic subculture. Outsiders—all outsiders—are considered prey who can be lied to, cheated, frightened, robbed and murdered.... Selling narcotics to strangers is business to the mafiosi, except when it threatens their homes." "The Story of T," *New York Times Magazine*, March 29, 1970, p. 13. Carlo Sforza, *The Real Italians: A Study in European Psychology* (New York: Columbia University Press, 1942), p. 56, comments upon the same phenomenon: "The home is loved in Italy, not for itself, but as a symbol of the continuity of the family. Even the most modest peasant hovel is an island among many other islands. Only at family feasts—births or marriages—does one lower the bridge between house and house and then only briefly. Yet this implies nothing like oriental seclusion. The Italians, like the ancient Greeks, feel that they were born for the market place; they are not eaten by the desire for solitude which often besets the Briton or the Scot. Thousands of years of city life together have taught every Italian the art of remaining alone in the midst of the noisy crowd; alone—of course, in the Italian sense of the word—with his wife and children. That is, by the way, the source of the Italian art of living together in harmony, three or four sons under the same roof in farm or palace."

2. Barzini, *The Italians*, p. 268.
3. Asturias, *El señor presidente*, pp. 125–26.
4. Williamson, *Culture and Policy*, p. 17.

5. An anthropological exposition of this fact can be found in Díaz, *Tonalá*, pp. 76–79. A parish priest in Spain speaks of "the quite undeniable fact, as far as Andalusia is concerned, that men consider the church a 'woman's affair' . . . and by and large leave churchgoing to the women." Fraser, *The Pueblo*, p. 114.

6. Evelyn P. Stevens, "Marianismo: The Other Face of Machismo in Latin America" (Paper prepared for meeting of Latin American Studies Association, Austin, Texas, December 1971), defines *marianismo* as "the cult of feminine spiritual superiority" (p. 3) which extends to every social class. It is possible, she says, "to regard marianismo as part of a reciprocal arrangement, the other half of which is *machismo*" (p. 21).

7. Bryan, *Improbable Irish*, p. 159.

8. *Life without Principle* (1863), from Carl Bode, ed., *The Portable Thoreau* (New York: Viking Press, 1947), p. 650.

9. *Selected Writings of Bolívar*, p. 291.

10. From a speech by Castro in Alice L. Hageman and Philip E. Wheaton, eds., *Religion in Cuba Today* (New York: Association Press, 1971), p. 136.

11. This concept should not be confused with the "two swords" theory of the medieval world. For a lucid exposition of the latter, see George H. Sabine, *A History of Political Theory* (New York: Holt, Rinehart, & Winston, 1961), pp. 194–96.

12. Saint Thomas Aquinas, *De regimine principum*, bk. 1, chap. 14.

13. Menéndez Pidal, *Spaniards in Their History*, p. 41. Or, as the old man in Fuentes, *Death of Artemio Cruz*, p. 38, says: "One must make distinctions. . . . Business, for example, is one thing, and religion is another."

14. Cited in Samuel Guy Inman, *Latin America: Its Place in World Life* (New York: Harcourt, Brace, 1942), p. 422.

15. For a discussion of the classical, biblical, and Stoic origins of the theory of the Two Cities, see the excellent introduction by Ernest Barker to Saint Augustine, *The City of God* (New York: Dutton, 1945), vol. 1.

16. Saint Augustine, *The City of God*, trans. Marcus Dods (New York: Modern Library, 1950), p. 477.

17. Ibid., pp. 607, 660.

18. Ibid., p. 680.

19. Ibid., p. 479. Cain's association with the Earthly City is as old as Augustine and as new as Rolf Hochhuth's *The Deputy* (New York: Grove Press, 1964). In that play, p. 148, the Cardinal says:

Was not even Cain, who killed his brother,
the instrument of God? Cain said to the Lord:
my sin is too great ever to be forgiven.
And still, you know, God set a mark on Cain
so that no one who came upon him would ever kill him.
What is it your Luther says:
secular rule derives from Cain, you know.
Cain had his mission in the world, as Noah did.
What can we know
of the terrible detours of the Lord!

20. Saint Augustine, *Enarrationes in Psalmos*, 51, 6.

21. This division of ethical precepts was never accepted by the Eastern Church, however. Following is a passage from Zoe Oldenbourg's *The Crusades* (New York: Ballantine Books, 1966), pp. 89–90, which throws light on the matter:

"The deep, irreconcilable difference between the traditions of Rome and Byzantium lay in the attitude of both to murder, or to war. This was something which emerged from the Crusades and it was more than a detail, more than just a matter of emphasis. Both were Christian, and both made war as a matter of course, celebrated their triumphs, prayed to God to grant them victory, and charged into battle carrying crosses and banners bearing the images of the saints. But for the Greeks no war, however "holy," could ever be anything but a sin, something concerning men alone. It was a venial and even a necessary sin, but a sin all the same, and sufficiently serious for a soldier of any kind, however just the war in which he was fighting, to be excluded from participating in the sacraments for at least some time as a penance. Bloodshed of any kind—even when the blood belonged to God's enemies—could on no account be looked on as virtuous. Like the good thief on Calvary, the most that any hero who fell fighting the Turks could hope for was a pardon *in extremis*, if he had the time to confess.

"In theory things were exactly the same in the West: Christian doctrine was explicit on such matters. However, from the middle of the eleventh century onward the popes had begun granting special indulgences to soldiers who were going to fight the Moors in Spain or placing themselves directly in the service of the Church, so that murder, under its noble name of war, had long enjoyed a strong prejudice in its favor. The secular ruling class was a military class and consequently its intellectual and ethical values were military values, a state of affairs against which the Church struggled in vain. Despite constant threats of excommunication, God's truce and God's peace were observed only by a small minority of knights, and understandably the Church could not condemn those who were fighting to defend her. She could only encourage the Spanish Christians in their efforts to win back their lands from the Moslems. Although the Emperor, the temporal head of the Byzantine Church, was also the head of the army, the Church herself, while granting her blessing to those waging a 'just' war, remained on one side, faithful in principle to her horror of all bloodshed. The Greeks would have been appalled to see their archbishop mounted on a battle charger, a helmet on his head and a sword in his hand, but we know the Latins, at least the knights, were by no means dismayed by such a sight.

"The fundamental difference lay in the coexistence in the Western mind of two quite separate ideals, the warrior and the Christian. Byzantium never seems to have been affected by any such ambivalence: it was too blatantly paradoxical for the logical Greek mind to accept."

22. See, for example, Edmund S. Morgan, *Visible Saints: The History of a Puritan Idea* (Ithaca, N.Y.: Cornell University Press, 1963).

23. On the contrasting attitudes toward church buildings of Protestants and Catholics, see William Pauck, *The Heritage of the Reformation* (New York: Oxford University Press, 1950), pp. 213–14.

24. "Luther was doing something new in affirming the inherently religious character of everyday life as the Christian is called by God to live it: the concept of

the Calling had not been so interpreted before." J. S. Whale, *The Protestant Tradition* (New York: Cambridge University Press, 1959), p. 109.

25. James Allen, *New England's Choicest Blessing* (Boston, 1679), p. 11.

26. "Whether it is a question of the doctrine of beatitude or the Blessed Trinity of the Eternal Law, of virtues and gifts, of contemplation, evil, divine providence and foreknowledge, predestination, and, generally, the whole field of sacred theology, there is nothing more obvious than St. Thomas's perfect fidelity to St. Augustine in his theological synthesis....

"The more one studies both of these Doctors, the better is Father Gardeil's statement verified: 'The positions on which they differ may be counted; it is impossible to number those in which they agree.... The dumb ox...has devoured the whole spiritual substance of the eagle of Hippo...he has made it, as much as Aristotle, the very substance of his own mind.' If the *essential* values of Augustine's thought be considered in their integrity, it must be admitted, as we have already shown, that the sole metaphysical systematization of this thought which remains *essentially* Augustinian is the Thomist synthesis." Jacques Maritain, "St. Augustine and St. Thomas Aquinas," in M. C. D'Arcy et al., *St. Augustine* (New York: Meridian, 1957), pp. 215, 218.

27. "...the XIIIth century, a century which, at certain moments, appears among the most irreligious in the history of Christianity." Guiseppe Toffanin, *History of Humanism* (New York: Las Americas, 1954), p. 11.

28. "The reality of the sacrament," said Aquinas, "is the unity of the mystical body, without which there can be no salvation; for there is no entering into salvation outside the Church." *Summa theologica*, 3.73.3. Sheldon S. Wolin, *Politics and Vision* (Boston: Little, Brown, 1960), p. 132, treats of this matter.

29. According to Powicke, even by Gregory VII's time "the visible Church on earth, under the guidance of the Pope, had become the accepted embodiment of the City of God, carrying with it all the high responsibilities which the maintenance of the divine order involved. Henceforth the Church set its face against any distinction between the Church visible and invisible." F. M. Powicke, "The Christian Life," in C. G. Crump and E. F. Jacob, eds., *Legacy of the Middle Ages* (Oxford: Clarendon Press, 1926), p. 50. This came about in no small part due to the contributions of Saint Augustine, as has been shown: "Later generations, who used the great work in apology or polemic, did not hesitate to see in the Church on earth a part of the Divine Society, having its own rules, structure, and catholic organization; and to this view Augustine's own doctrine of the sacraments, his whole construction of the foundations of other Christian dogma, had perhaps already made the greatest contribution. Through him, more than through any other, the Church came to regard herself as a great organized body holding out to man the *scala perfectionis* by which he could ascend from the Babylon of worldly existence to the Heavenly Jerusalem." E. F. Jacob, "Political Thought," in Crump and Jacob, *Legacy of the Middle Ages*, p. 513.

30. "The office proper to a priest is to be a mediator between God and the people." Aquinas, *Summa theologica*, 3.22.1, 3. For a critical view, see Miguel de Unamuno, *Tragic Sense of Life* (New York: Dover, 1954), chap. 4.

31. Fyodor Dostoevsky, putting words into the mouth of the elder at the monastery, gives one a feeling for the power of repentance: "Fear nothing and never

be afraid; and don't fret. If only your penitence fail not, God will forgive all. There is no sin, and there can be no sin on all the earth, which the Lord will not forgive to the truly repentant! Man cannot commit a sin so great as to exhaust the infinite love of God. Can there be a sin which could exceed the love of God? Think only of repentance, continual repentance, but dismiss fear altogether. Believe that God loves you as you cannot conceive; that He loves you with your sin, in your sin. It has been said of old that over one repentant sinner there is more joy in heaven than over ten righteous men. Go, and fear not." *The Brothers Karamazov* (New York: Modern Library, 1950), p. 57. Graham Greene, in *The Power and the Glory* (New York: Bantam Books, 1954), p. 24, captures the conventional belief in God's forgiveness for sins of the world. According to his Padre José, "some mad renegade Catholic, puffed up with the Governor's politics, had once broken into a church and seized the Host. He had spat on it, trampled it, and then the people had got him and hanged him as they did the stuffed Judas on Holy Thursday from the belfry. He wasn't so bad a man, Padre José thought—he would be forgiven, he was just a politician." Or, as Machiavelli wrote, "I believe, have believed, and will always believe that it is true, as Boccaccio said, that it is better to act and repent than not to act and repent." "Familiar Letters," in Gilbert, *Machiavelli: The Chief Works*, 2: 941. See also Machiavelli, "An Exhortation on Penitence," ibid., 1: 170-71.

32. The sacrament, however, was not in the hands of equals. While in theory the clergy might be quite equal to the participants in the Mass, in fact, the ecclesiastical law through its *jus divinum* which referred to the position rather than the person of the priest as an intermediary of salvation was blurred in practice. With the elevation of the sacraments in the Church, the position of the priests was also elevated. Communal life of primitive Christianity had given way to a distinct division between clergy and laity.

33. William J. Coleman, *Latin-American Catholicism: A Self-Evaluation* (Maryknoll, N.Y.: Maryknoll Publications, 1958), p. 20. This idea was embodied in Machiavelli's observation that "the nearer people are to the Church of Rome which is the head of our religion, the less religious are they." *Discorsi*, p. 165. Luther was so incensed by the infidelity of Romans that he sought to abolish all pilgrimages. In passing he parallels Machiavelli's statement when he notes that "the Romanists themselves have coined the saying, 'The nearer Rome, the worse the Christians.' " "An Appeal to the Ruling Class," in Dillenberger, *Martin Luther*, p. 443.

34. "Skepticism is common among laymen, at least on the verbal level, and laymen on the whole do not participate actively in ordinary Church affairs other than fiestas and sodalities. Regular confession, attendance at mass, and the like, are often left mainly to women.... Few persons are, however, willing to sever connections with the Church entirely or to forego its intervention for the salvation of their souls. Opposition centers mainly about the Church's place in secular affairs." John P. Gillin, "Mestizo America," in Ralph Linton, ed., *Most of the World* (New York: Columbia University Press, 1949), pp. 208-9. Simón Bolívar, in 1822, chastized the bishop of Popayán (Colombia) for meddling in politics and demonstrated his concern for "the universality of the Church of Rome," pointing out that "the responsibility for this terrible separation would

fall particularly upon those who, though able to maintain the unity of the Church of Rome, have, by their negative conduct, hastened the greatest of evils, namely ·the ruin of the Church and the death of souls through all eternity" *Selected Writings of Bolívar*, p. 292.

35. H. Richard Niebuhr, *Christ and Culture* (New York: Harper, 1951), p. 146. Huizinga supported this interpretation. Toward the end of the medieval period, he writes, "the spirit of the Middle Ages, still plastic and naive, longs to give concrete shape to every conception. Every thought seeks expression in an image, but in this image it solidifies and becomes rigid. By this tendency to embodiment in visible forms all holy concepts are constantly exposed to the danger of hardening into mere externalism." Johan Huizinga, *The Waning of the Middle Ages* (Garden City, N.Y.: Doubleday, 1954), p. 152.

36. Ferdinand Schevill, "The Society of the Italian Renaissance," in James W. Thompson, et al., *The Civilization of the Renaissance* (Chicago: University of Chicago Press, 1929), p. 60.

37. Wolin, *Politics and Vision*, chap. 7, has suggested the reverse.

38. Official Catholicism has not been anxious to claim its offspring. Machiavelli's works were placed on the Index in 1551. In 1576 appeared the *Discours sur les moyens de bien gouverner et maintenir en bonne paix un royaume autre principaute, divises en trois livres, à savoir du conseil, de la religion, et police que doit tenir un prince. Contra Nicolas Machiavel Florentin*, popularly known as the *Anti-Machiavel*. This broadside was directed against the religious doctrines of Machiavelli—his alleged atheism. See Henri Busson, *Le rationalisme dans la littérature française de la Renaissance (1533-1601)* (Paris: Librairie Philosophique J. Vrin, 1957), pp. 562-63.

39. Friedrich Meinecke, *Machiavellism: The Doctrine of Raison d'Etat and Its Place in Modern History* (New York: Praeger, 1957), p. 39.

40. Martin Luther, "Secular Authority: To What Extent It Should Be Obeyed," in Dillenberger, *Martin Luther*, p. 368.

41. Ernesto Landi, "Machiavelli," p. 43.

42. Machiavelli, *Il principe*, p. 70.

43. Cassirer does not see the significance of this fact when he says that it remains "one of the great puzzles in the history of human civilization how a man like Machiavelli, a ·great and noble mind, could become the advocate of 'splendid wickedness.'" Ernst Cassirer, *The Myth of the State* (New Haven: Yale University Press, 1946), p. 145. Machiavelli is not advocating "splendid wickedness." He only says that there are two cities and that there must be two moralities. Saint Thomas, in essence, had made the same argument.

It is interesting to note in this regard the neoscholastic response to Machiavelli. Neoscholastics attack Machiavelli for maintaining that there are these two distinct and politically antithetical moralities. Following Aquinas, they believe Machiavelli failed to appreciate that one can explain the fact and necessity of evil and still stay within one's system of virtue. For example, one neoscholastic political scientist says: "There is to be noted here that complication which Jacques Maritain has pointed out. It is the complication arising from Machiavelli's 'rough and elementary idea of moral science,' which makes him fail to understand its 'realist, experiential . . . character. Accordingly, what he calls vice and evil, and considers to be contrary to virtue and morality, may sometimes be only the authentically moral behavior of a just man engaged in the complexities of human life and of true ethics.' " Charles N. R. McCoy, *The Structure of Political Thought* (New York: McGraw-Hill, 1963), p. 171. Neoscholastics are stating what Aquinas would have said; that the "authentically moral behavior of a just man" engaging in the complexities of human life when pursuing the common good may sometimes have to use expediential or evil means. That is, acting publicly, the Christian man has to draw upon the values of the Earthly City. The difference between Thomism and Machiavellianism, in this sense, is small indeed. Consider, for example, Donald W. Bleznick, "Spanish Reaction to Machiavelli in the Sixteenth and Seventeenth Centuries," *Journal of the History of Ideas* 19 (1958): 542–50, and Pedro de Rivadeneyra, S.J., *Tratado de la religión y virtudes que debe tener el príncipe cristiano para gobernar y conservar sus estados. Contra lo que Nicolas Maquiavelo y los políticos desde tiempe enseñan* (Madrid: Biblioteca de Autores Españoles, 1868), vol. 60.

44. R. M. Morse in a perceptive article notes the same problem in Latin America. The swing, he says is between Thomism and Machiavellianism. However, he, as have others, fails to see the basic compatibility of the two. Richard M. Morse, "Toward a Theory of Spanish American Government," *Journal of the History of Ideas* 15 (1954): 71–93.

45. "He spoke and judged from his own personal experience." Cassirer, *Myth of the State*, pp. 140–41; "Only ambiguously do we express the difference between the thought of Machiavelli and that of most men in the Middle Ages, or in the 16th century, when we say that he separated ethics from politics." "It was, roughly speaking, on this principle that Italian politics had long been conducted." J. W. Allen, *A History of Political Thought in the Sixteenth Century* (London: Methuen, 1928), pp. 472, 476; "Machiavelli *lifted into consciousness* this ethos of his time." Jacques Maritain, *The Range of Reason* (New York: Scribner's, 1952), p. 135; "Even if the statesmen themselves learnt nothing new from it..." Meinecke, *Machiavellism*, p. 39.

46. Maritain, *The Range of Reason*, p. 139.

47. Allan H. Gilbert, *Machiavelli's Prince and Its Forerunners: The Prince as a Typical Book de Regimine Principum* (Durham, N.C.: Duke University Press, 1938). It is true, however, that Catholic Christians ever since Saint Augustine have been enamored with the works of that most famous of Romans, Cicero. Aquinas, Machiavelli, and Bolívar uniformly sprinkle their writings with references to him. And although traditional Christian theology denied the premise, there has been a constant tendency to believe with Cicero (see especially his Dream of Scipio) that man is rewarded in the next world for the great public deeds which he oversees here on earth. Thus Catholic man is not only freed from undue concern over the future of his soul by immoral public acts but also intuits that the success of his public career may lead toward eternal reward.

48. Sindulfo Pérez M. and Carlos Meo, *Stroessner* (Asunción: Offset Gráfica Asuncena, 1972), pp. 116–21. The wisdom of Machiavelli has been consistently esteemed in Latin America. For example, the Supreme Junta of Bogotá (Sep-

tember 25, 1810), noting the royalists' actions in Quito proclaimed "¡Alerta ciudadanos de Santafé! Que este ejemplar os enseñe a ser más cautos, menos confiados, y más atentos a la política de Maquiavelo!" Eduardo Posada, *El 20 de julio* (Bogotá: Biblioteca de Historia Nacional, 1914), p. 265.

49. Leo Strauss, *Thoughts on Machiavelli* (Glencoe, Ill.: Free Press, 1959), p. 10. Machiavelli's own words, "I love my native city more than my soul." From a letter to Francesco Vettori (1527), reprinted in Gilbert, *Machiavelli: The Chief Works*, 2: 1010. This quote from Machiavelli is cited by Max Weber, *Protestant Ethic*, p. 107, as being in sharpest contrast with the otherworldliness of Protestants. Weber, however, fails to note the particular Catholic nature of Machiavelli's statement. In his essay, "Politics as a Vocation," it appears to me Weber has gone beyond the objectivity he so cherished. In discussing the issue anew, he utilizes Machiavelli to support his own non-Christian bias. See *From Max Weber: Essays in Sociology* (New York: Oxford University Press, 1946), pp. 125–28.

50. Cited in Roberto Ridolfi, *The Life of Niccolò Machiavelli*, trans. Cecil Grayson (Chicago: University of Chicago Press, 1963), p. 250.

51. Meinecke, *Machiavellism*, p. 29.

52. Nor among Renaissance public men was Machiavelli alone in this dualism. One writer has been prompted to exclaim: "Lived like heathens and died like Christians—was applicable to very many of the representatives of the new classical culture." Cited by Reinhold Seeberg, *Textbook of the History of Doctrines* (Grand Rapids, Mich.: Baker Book House, 1952), 2: 215.

It may be relevant to note that the same kind of pragmatism pervades Catholic society today in its so-called deviant forms, namely Latin American Communism. A friend used to remark cynically that 90 percent of the Communists in Guatemala could be rounded up by a simple expedient of arresting everyone who took part in the annual Good Friday parade through Guatemala City. Communism and Christianity are seldom seen as antithetical movements in caudillaje culture. Matthews, *Fidel Castro*, p. 36, reports that "an old Cuban Government official and a friend of Castro's was dying. Castro visited him and it was Fidel who said to him: 'But you must have Monsignor Zacchi (the Vatican Chargé d'Affaires) to come in and give you the last sacraments.'"

53. "Familiar Letters," in Gilbert, *Machiavelli: The Chief Works*, vol. 2. On church attendance, see p. 973.

54. Ibid., p. 973. Speaking of "our archbishop" whom he presumes dead, Machiavelli says "may God receive his soul" (p. 901). His letters usually begin with a "Jesus Son of Mary" (p. 903) and often end with a traditional "Christ keep you," "Christ watch over you," or "Christ guard you."

The famous Benvenuto Cellini, a hard-living worldly sculptor and goldsmith of Machiavelli's time wrote that while in prison he said to the guard, "the sooner I escape from this earthly prison, the happier shall I be; especially as I am sure my soul is saved, and that I am going to an undeserved death. Christ, the glorious and divine, elects me to the company of His disciples and friends, who, like Himself, were condemned to die unjustly." *Autobiography of Benvenuto Cellini*, trans. John Addington Symonds (Garden City, N.Y.: Doubleday, 1961), p. 269. It should also be recalled that Pico Mirandola and Marsilio Ficino, two celebrated humanists, both received holy orders into the

Church before their deaths. Cecilia M. Ady, *Lorenzo dei Medici and Renaissance Italy* (New York: Collier, 1962), p. 114.

Machiavelli's well-known contemporary, Francesco Guicciardini, held to the same Catholic dualism. As stated by Luigi Barzini: "What is striking and instructive about Messer Francesco is the wide discrepancy between his personal thoughts and beliefs, and his public acts. What is even more striking and instructive is the fact that he was not surprised or troubled by the discrepancy which he placidly accepted as one of the facts of life. He never allowed his private intimate convictions to interfere with the business on hand. He was, for instance, privately a devoted and religious man, honest and honourable, brought up strictly within the Catholic faith. In his youth he had even thought of becoming a priest." *The Italians*, p. 169.

In a new version of Machiavelli's familiar lines about loving his native city, Guicciardini defends his public support of a papal establishment which he hated: "My position under several Popes has compelled me to desire their aggrandisement for the sake of my own profit. Otherwise, I should have loved Martin Luther like myself—not that I might break loose from the laws which Christianity...imposes on us, but that I might see...villains... forced to live either without vices or without power." Francesco Guicciardini, *Ricordi politici e civili* (Turin: Unione Tipografico-Editrice Torinese, 1926), no. 346.

55. It is indicative that Machiavelli praised Ferdinand of Aragon, king of all Spain, as a model of the "new prince," who "has become for fame and glory the first king of Christendom, and if you regard his actions you will find them all very great and some of them extraordinary." *Il principe*, chap. 21. Needless to say, Machiavelli was not speaking of the "Christian morality" of Ferdinand.

56. Here in the New World was enacted on a massive scale a manner of sin and absolution that regularly, if on a more selective basis, took place in the Old. "At Milan the Duke Giovan Maria Visconti (1412) was assassinated at the entrance of the church of San Gottardo, Galeazzo Maria Sforza (1476) in the church of Santo Stefano , and Lodovico el Moro only escaped (1484) the daggers of the adherents of the widowed Duchess Bona, through entering the church of Sant' Ambrogio by another door than that by which he was expected. There was no intentional impiety in the act; the assassins of Galeazzo did not fail to pray before the murder to the patron saint of the church, and to listen devoutly to the first mass." Jacob Burckhardt, *The Civilization of the Renaissance in Italy* (New York: Modern Library, 1954), p. 47.

57. Morse astutely observes the two sides of the Latin American character (e.g., "Spanish conquistadors, colonizers and catechizers, then, carried with them to American shores this dual heritage: medieval and Renaissance, Thomistic and Machiavellian"). What he does not perceive is that the heritage is singular, the ethic is dual. Morse, "Toward a Theory," pp. 71–93.

58. Dante, *De monarchia*, bk. 3, chap. 16.

59. On the religious affiliation of these men, see J. Lloyd Mecham, *Church and State in Latin America* (Chapel Hill: University of North Carolina Press, 1934), pp. 51ff. The continued importance of the "heavenly" city in Latin America is obvious. While Orlando Fals-Borda seems to miss the implications of this fact, his discussion of what he calls "The Ethic of Other-Worldliness"

is worthwhile. See "Violence and the Break-up of Tradition in Colombia," in Claudio Véliz, ed., *Obstacles to Change in Latin America* (London: Oxford University Press, 1969), pp. 189, 193ff.

60. Santos, "Personal Values," p. 10.

61. *Selected Writings of Bolívar*, p. 604. Kenneth Underwood has found this same dualism among Catholic leaders in a North American city: "Since the Roman Catholic leaders start their interpretations of politics from the most systematically and precisely developed metaphysical and ethical position of all the religious groups, they give the greatest attention to efforts to define the 'religious and non-religious issues' and the 'moral and technical aspects' of problems faced by politicians. Even though the Roman Catholic leaders differ at times in their demarcation of the boundaries, they are diligent in their attempts to maintain and observe distinctions between the spiritual and political spheres." Kenneth W. Underwood, *Protestant and Catholic: Religious and Social Integration in an Industrial Community* (Boston: Beacon Press, 1957), p. 304. A good example of the success of this dualism within the United States can be found in the life of that Irish Catholic leader, Mayor Daley. Mike Royko, *Boss: Richard J. Daley of Chicago* (New York: New American Library, 1971), p. 13 and passim.

62. Hageman and Wheaton, *Religion in Cuba Today*, p. 132.

63. Such a separation makes perfectly consistent an argument either (1) for Catholicism as a state religion, or (2) for the separation of Church and State. Bolívar and Castro as well as a host of lesser figures favored the latter. "God and his ministers are the authorities on religion," said Bolívar, "and religion exerts its influence solely through spiritual means and bodies, never through instruments of the nation's body politic, which serves only to direct public energies toward purely temporal ends." *Selected Writings of Bolívar*, p. 605.

On the other hand, caudillaje men could seek to make Catholicism the official state religion—as every Latin American constitution of the independence era did—because all believed, including Bolívar, and Castro today, in the truths of Catholicism as they pertain to the private sphere. For example, in championing the separation of Church and State, Bolívar was *not* arguing for religious diversity. On the contrary, he said, "the spiritual pastors are obliged to teach the gospel of Heaven. The example of all the true disciples of Christ is the eloquent teacher of his divine doctrine.... it would seem to me ... to be sacrilegious and profane for us to interfere with the Commandments of the Lord by enactments of our own" (ibid.). When the rightist Spanish Falange in the 1930s sought to exclude the Church from secular matters, controversy followed. Party leader Primo de Rivera, however, had assured the members that "the Catholic interpretation of life is first of all, the true one; but historically, moreover, it is the Spanish one.... Accordingly, any reconstruction of Spain must be in a Catholic sense." José Antoñio Primo de Rivera, *The Spanish Answer*, trans. Juan M. Calder (Madrid: Artes Gráficas Ibarra, 1964), p. 66.

INDEX

Library of Congress Cataloging in Publication Data

Dealy, Glen Caudill.

The public man.

Includes bibliographical references and index.

1. Latin America—Civilization—1948–

2. Catholic Church—Influence. I. Title.

F1414.2.D37   980   77-1423

ISBN 0-87023-239-8